THE U.S.A.: AN AERIAL CLOSE-UP

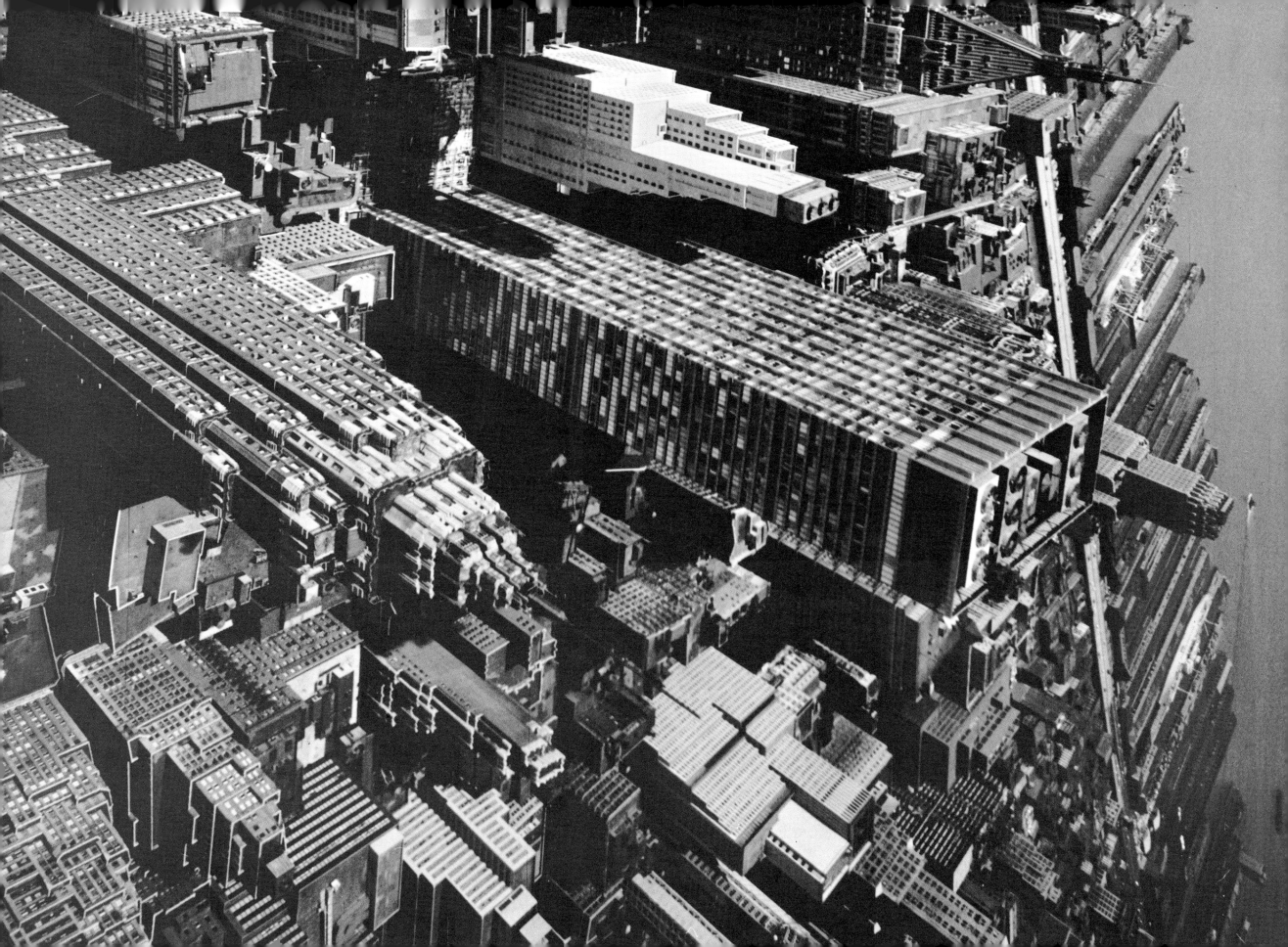

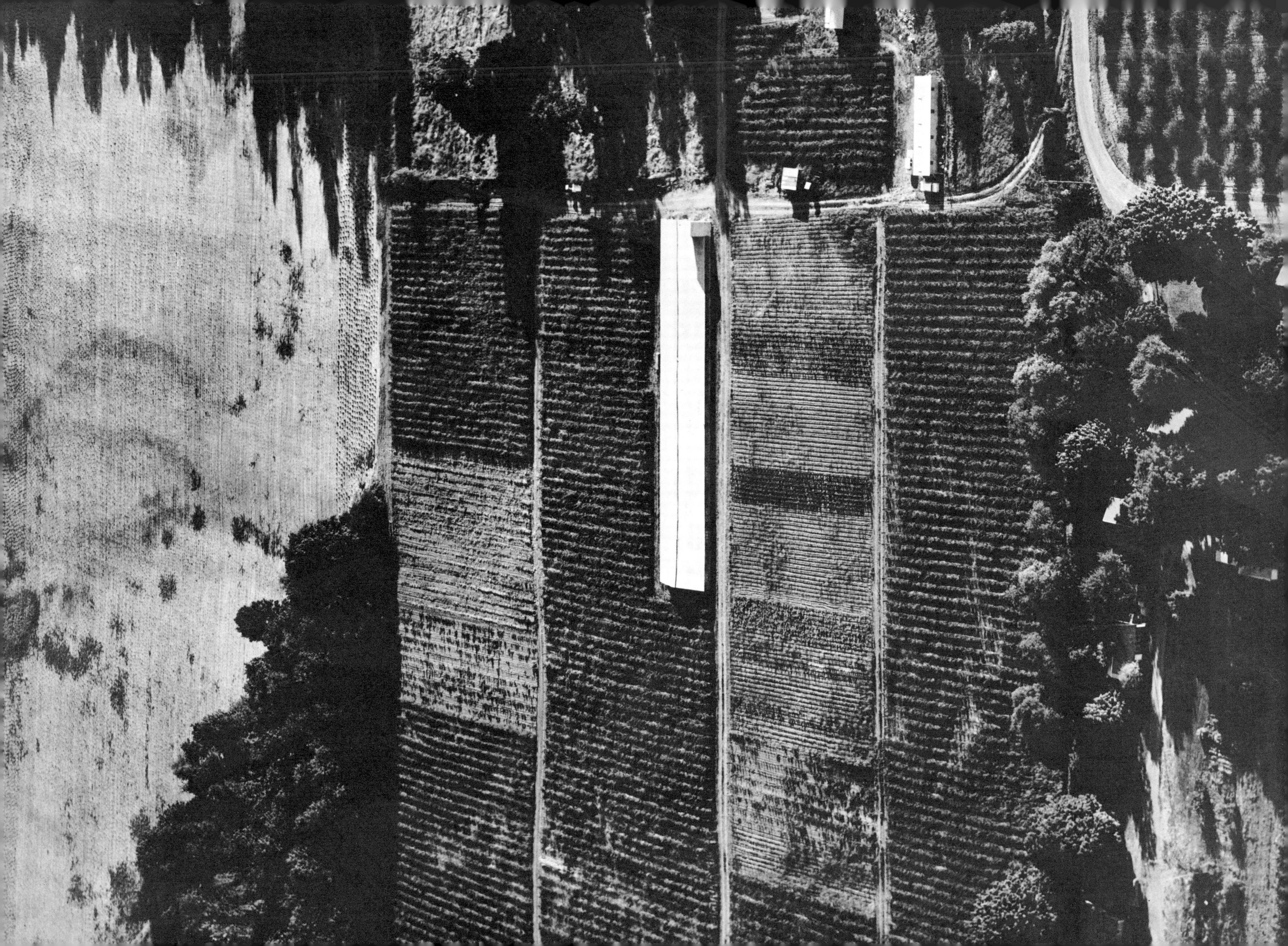

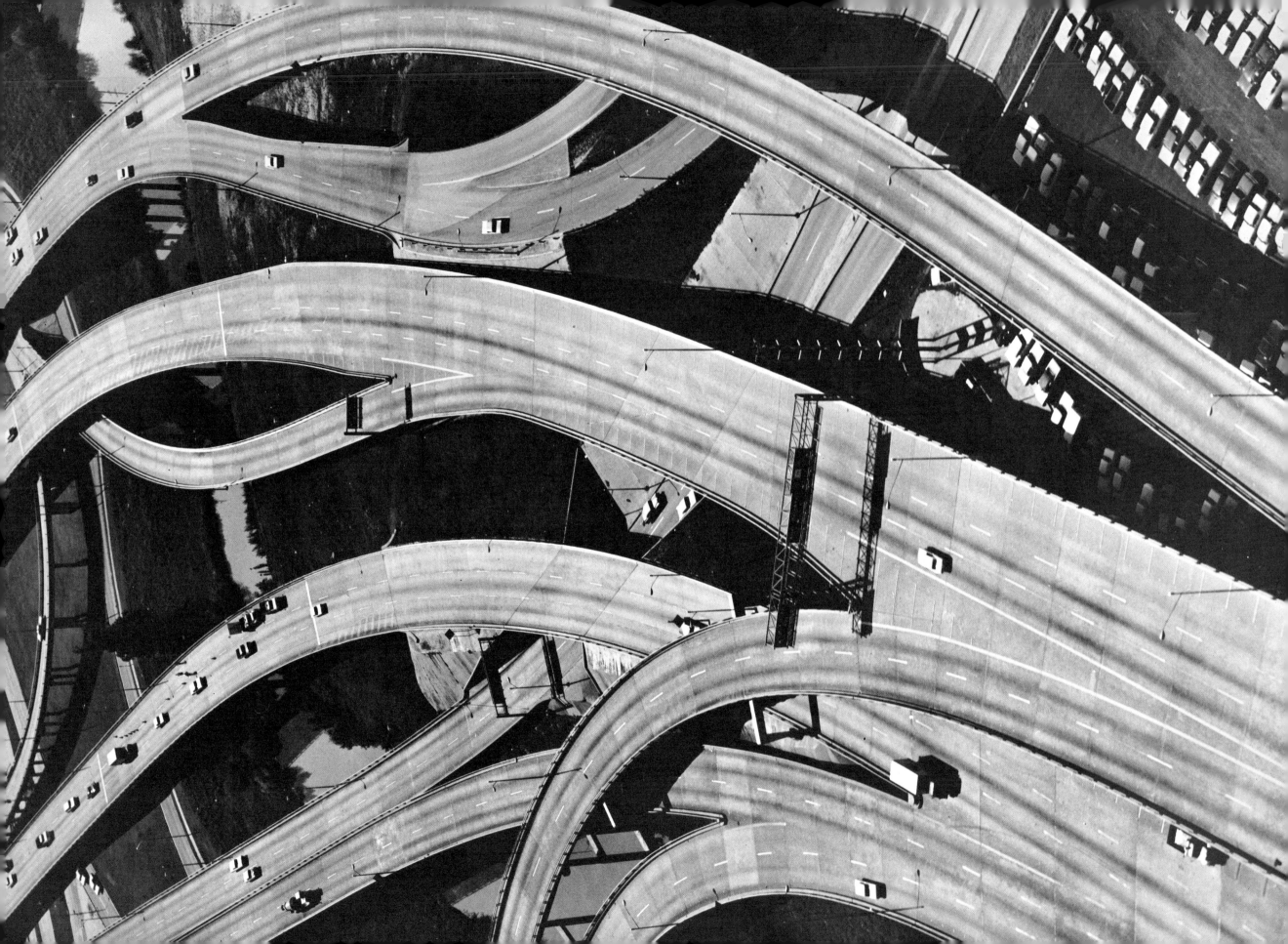

The U.S.A.

An Aerial Close-up

BY CHARLES E. ROTKIN

CROWN PUBLISHERS, INC., NEW YORK

Library of Congress Catalog Card Number 68–23450

Book Design by Adele D. Rotkin

Consulting Book Designer, Lenni Schur

Consulting Picture Editor, Cornell Capa

Printed in the United States of America
First Edition

CONTENTS

ATLANTA STADIUM jammed with 60,000 spectators at a professional football game.

PHOTOGRAPHER–AUTHOR Charles E. Rotkin on assignment at a railroad yard in Texas. The camera he is using here is a much modified U.S. Navy F–8 and is the same one used to make many of the photographs appearing in this book.

SOME READERS OF THIS VOLUME may have seen an earlier work of mine, *Europe: An Aerial Close-up*, and recall the incredible impositions put on the aerial photographer for choosing Europe as his subject. To those not familiar with that book, let me briefly state that making aerial photographs in Europe is beset by a bureaucracy developed to the highest degree known to man. With few exceptions, all such activity is rigidly controlled by a spiderweb of officialdom not only requiring different permits for photographing every square centimeter of European earth but also restricting one's freedom by even limiting the number of pieces of film used.

What pure joy, therefore, to work in the United States, where such idiotic limitations do not exist. With the exception of some military posts, there are no restrictions as to subject. But while the freedom of movement we have here is great and limitless, the very size of the United States presents problems that do not exist in Western Europe.

Where does one begin and where does one end? The United States is measurable (3,615,211 square miles), the population has turned the 200 million mark, and the once-familiar forty-eight states are now fifty. How many cities are there? How many do we photograph? Any serious photographic coverage of the United States must always be an intensively subjective one, and so we have here not a geography, history, topographic map, or a visual atlas, but a personal statement from low-flying helicopters and other small aircraft of what I saw and liked (and a few things I didn't).

Not every city is represented, nor is every state, and so some may be insulted by the omission of their communities. Alaska had to be by-passed because of the logistics of getting there, and covering it properly would have thrown our whole schedule out of balance. Also, personal taste is always a factor, and I liked some places better than others. In a country this large, there are many, many similar-looking areas. Only after decades of neglect are America's cities beginning to show signs of originality in their redevelopment and new architecture. But far too many of them are still wall-to-wall parking lots and block after block of nondescript buildings.

Curiously enough, slums often do not look like slums from the air, except for the unrelieved monotony. What is apparent, however, almost everywhere are the heaps of just plain junk piled up in backyards, thrown into ravines, or buried behind factory buildings. The rural areas are no exception. More often than once what appeared to be a lovely village turned out on closer approach to be a warren of cluttered gas stations or used-car lots; or the fields frequently hid discarded farm equipment or car carcasses.

Some of these photographs were made on assignment, and a few are included for purely nostalgic reasons, such as the railroad roundhouse at El Reno, Oklahoma (page 121), the water hole (page 115), and the farm (pages 116–117). True, the roundhouse is long gone and the busy yards are now trafficked by rumbling diesels. Today's or tomorrow's fathers may be hard pressed to answer the question of "Daddy, what's a roundhouse?"

As for the farms, aside from the sprouting of TV antennas, time, from all outward appearances, seems to have stood still.

Driving about the country this way is essentially a lonely business. Over the years I have made many friends, and their cities always became welcome oases. I have heard it said that one's assessment of a city is finally based upon the people one knows or meets there, not by its landmarks, restaurants, or saloons. Therefore, when I speak fondly of Seattle or San Francisco or New Orleans, these feelings are not generated by the sights, sounds, and smells, but by the people I met and got to know because they, rather than the landmarks, come to mind first.

Thus I developed a special fondness for western Wyoming because a master mechanic named Paul Bradshaw not only towed me to safety after a motor breakdown thirty miles west of nowhere but also spent half the night fixing my car, and then refused to accept a penny for his services.

I met many such selfless people on these trips, like Dwight Calkins, a farm-machinery distributor from Spokane who took the time to fly me in his own plane around the Grand Coulee area; or, on the lighter side, a charming lady with the improbable name of Margaret Savage Love who not only graciously toured me around the Taos Pueblo at the request of a mutual friend but also capped the tour with a picnic hamper and a shaker of ice-cold martinis.

There were other light moments, too. While photographing the Mississippi River above New Orleans one warm fall day, what better way to enjoy a box lunch, complete with gleaming silverware and bright linen, prepared by the Chef of the Royal Orleans Hotel, than to set our helicopter down on the levee, dine by the riverside, then lift off and continue shooting.

For low-level aerial photography the helicopter is an amazing camera platform, and, because of urban congestion, only with it can certain kinds of photographs be made. This was not the case twenty-odd years ago when I started to shoot from light planes, such as the workhorse Piper J-3. Radios in planes were literally unheard of then, and you didn't get the idea that Big Brother was constantly watching you. By contrast, while using a more modern plane recently, every time we would line up on our subject, the tower operator of an airfield twenty miles away became almost hysterical because he could not find us on his radar. The fact that we were out over a coastal swamp made little difference to him. We were just one more blip on a too crowded radarscope.

Weather is always a factor on aerial assignments. But there were other factors that insisted on their own priority. Like time and tide, the wheat combiners wait for no photographer. And there were many unpredictable situations such as a state-owned helicopter preempted from under us so that the state attorney general could attend a local race riot.

Helicopters, unfortunately, are not always available everywhere, so I often flew with crop dusters, who are used to flying low and in tight patterns. In South Dakota my camera jammed and I could not free it while airborne, so the pilot casually dropped his duster into a pasture as easily as he would park his car at a supermarket. He knew the country intimately, and correctly predicted where we could flush a doe and her fawn from the scrub cover. I felt that the airplane had become an extension of his senses, and would respond automatically, even without his touching the controls.

As a photographer I have often felt that the camera functioned as an extension of my own thoughts, and nowhere was this more graphically demonstrated than when I was photographing Mount Rainier. As soon as we got above the pall of polluted air emanating from the pulp mills around Tacoma, I started shooting. In a few minutes I had made nearly fifty exposures with no recollection of having done so. Was it the fascination of the mountain, so close and so majestic, that allowed me to shoot so unconsciously? Or was it some of the challenge that makes men climb mountains, because I reacted similarly in the Mount Hood area. And after all, how many pictures could I really use of either mountain?

Among the costs of production, I want to explain one item that might be particularly puzzling to the Indians of the Taos Pueblo. As all tourists who have visited the pueblo know, there is a fifty-cent charge for making pictures, so if the Indians should find a Kennedy half-dollar nearby, I merely want to explain that I paid my fee by tossing it out of the airplane as we went by on our final pass.

We are indeed grateful for the gracious help we received from so many people and organizations around the country. Without it, the pure economics of covering such a vast area might have prevented the entire project from getting off the ground. It's quite difficult to assess the value of this assistance, some tangible, some intangible, and much of it beyond anything we might normally expect even in this world of public relations courtesies. Who is to measure the value of finding a hotel room—in a crowded southern city on a football Saturday, or the supreme hospitality of friends, or friends of friends, who opened their homes to me or called a key person in some local civic group?

A most enjoyable change of pace, too, was to move in, bag and baggage, as I did with photographer Bert Brandt and his family in Houston. Here was not only the opportunity to resupply, get a camera fixed, and collect mail, but a chance to relax, spend a weekend in small talk, cook a soufflé or an onion soup (as I seem to have done in several widely scattered areas from Alabama to Hawaii), and in general feel thoroughly at home until the time came to move on.

So many of these gestures helped pave the way that, rather than dedicate this book to any one person, I would like, as I did in EUROPE, to dedicate it to the many people who gave so freely of their time and efforts.

I am very grateful to Mr. James C. Gross, Executive Director of the National Association of Travel Organizations, and Mr. Robert E. Short, Chairman of the Discover America program, whose initial enthusiasm helped open many regional doors for me. And I particularly want to express my gratitude to the Bell Helicopter Company for providing their helicopters to enable me to take many of the photographs in this book.

Thanks also to the following people (and the organizations with which they are connected): Mr. Thomas C. Veale and Max Ewing of the Atlantic-Richfield Refining Company; Mr. Harold A. Swenson of the Philadelphia Visitors and Convention Bureau; Mr. James N. Morris of the Mobile Chamber of Commerce; Mrs. Marge Booker of the San Francisco Convention and Visitors Bureau, and Mr. W. K. Popham of the Olympic Hotel; Mr. Hartly H. Kruger of the Oakland Chamber of Commerce; Mr. Bill Hardman of the Georgia Department of Industry and Trade; Mr. Rosser E. Smith of the Savannah Chamber of Commerce; Mr. David B. Cowles of HCA's Savannah Inn and Country Club; Mr. Stuart Smith of the St. Petersburg City News Bureau; Mr. Lew Price of the City of Miami; Mr. Al Wolfe of the City of Miami Beach News Bureau; Mr. Mead Parce of the Jacksonville Chamber of Commerce; and Mrs. Kathryn Kearing and Mr. Troy Garrison of the P & O Lines.

In Hawaii, a special bow to Mrs. Dee Prather of the Hawaii Visitors Bureau and Mr. Johnny Peacock and his Royal Hawaiian Flying Service; Pat Patrick, helicopter pilot for KHVH in Honolulu; Jeri Bostwick of the Sheraton Hotels Corporation; Marge Studer of Inter-Island Resorts; and to Gil McCloy, Bob Alderman, and John Felix of the Hawaiian Civil Air Patrol for their guidance and cooperation. In Louisiana, Phil Brady of the New Orleans Convention Bureau and "Scoop" (no one dares call him anything but that) Kennedy of the Mayor's office; Mr. Willard Robertson; Mr. James E. Wilson of the Shell Oil Company; and Miss Marilyn Barnett of the Royal Orleans Hotel who inspired the picnic lunch on the banks of the Mississippi. And the very knowledgeable Clint Bolton who not only pinpointed many locations for me but whose vital knowledge of the watering holes along Bourbon Street makes it impossible for any friend of his to die of thirst.

Thanks also to Art Long of the Reno News Bureau; Jim Deitch and Don Payne of the Las Vegas News Bureau; Mr. Brigham Townsend of the Hotel Tropicana; and Bob Butcher, the local Avis man who did try harder. Meanwhile, back at the Ranchos de Taos, my thanks go to Mrs. Margo Grainger for arranging with Bill Miller to make his personal Cessna available to me; also to Bert Coleman of the Arizona State Development Board; Ken McClure of the Phoenix News Bureau; and Vic Fryer and Gene Kinney of the Oregon Highway Department.

My coverage of the State of Washington owes much to the efforts of Mrs. Hanna Reisner of the Seattle Visitors Bureau, Jay Becker, and Hank Pearson, and it gave me the opportunity of renewing a friendship of twenty years with Mrs. Beatrice Howell who, with her mother and aunt, provided my anchor point in the Northwest.

I want to express my appreciation also to the Minnesota Department of Business Development, and to Scott Benton, Deputy Commissioner; Milt Holman, and Minnesota Aviation Representative Jack Gautier; Mr. Gilbert Crandall and Lester Trott of the Maryland Department of Economic Development; and Sergeant Frank Hudson of the Maryland State Police; Mr. John Brennan, Promotion Director of the State of New Hampshire; Mr. R. J. Crowley, Jr., and Mr. Gordon Bunker of their Aviation Department; Mr. John D. Kretschmer of the State of South Carolina and Mr. Tom Longerbeam of the Charleston Chamber of Commerce; Mr. Paul Besselievre of the South Dakota Black Hills, Badlands and Lakes Association; Mr. Tony Bevinetto of the Wyoming Travel Commission; and Mr. Ben Gillespie of the Houston Chamber of Commerce.

In addition my thanks to Mr. Brooke Alexander, Assistant to the Publisher of Fortune magazine; Mr. A. B. C. Whipple and Mr. Earle Kersh of the International Editions of Life magazine for their cooperation; and the Public Relations Department of the Standard Oil Company (N.J.) for making readily available some photographs shot for them on assignments.

The black-and-white film was processed and the reproduction prints were made by Compo-Photo Color under the supervision of Dave Mintzer, Dick Shuler, Ernie Pile, and Mrs. Sybil Collins. The color was processed by K & L Color Service in New York and by Ramell, Inc., in San Francisco. Thanks also to Irwin Welcher and A. A. Kelly of General Graphics Service in San Francisco for the experimental processing on the night aerials. I am grateful to Miss Beverly Schanzer for the copy editing and to Mrs. Ann Metcalfe, Sally Teichman, and Judy Rothenberg for their assistance.

To all these people who gave so generously of their time, I say "Thank you," and hope these results justify all their efforts.

The Gateway States

TODAY THE IMMIGRANT to America is apt to arrive by air, and chances are he won't have to pass through New York's harbor at all. But for most of the millions who preceded him, as well as tourists and returning American travelers, New York's harbor, with the Statue of Liberty in the Upper Bay, will always be the symbol of America. Overworked as a symbol—perhaps—and now dwarfed in size by the soaring Verrazano-Narrows Bridge, nevertheless the sight of the beautiful lady with the torch always evokes deep feelings from the traveler seeing her against the great skyline. And when a new ship arrives in the harbor, greeted by tooting tugs and spraying fireboats, this traditional welcome is New York's unique way of saying, "Welcome to America!"

Since the beginning of this country, the eastern states from New England to Florida have always served as gateways for people and commodities. Name the ports from Boston to Philadel-

phia, south to Baltimore all the way down the coast to Savannah and Jacksonville—all have been active harbors and transportation centers. And though a few of them may exceed all the others in handling certain commodities, such as grain, coal, or iron ore (or even hummingbirds' tongues), it is the Port of New York that carries the mainstream of traffic.

The same must be said (with all the parochial feelings of a born New Yorker) of the City of New York. Bigger, more crowded, noisier, dirtier, and perhaps even uglier than any other, it is a city that has something for everyone. (I wish I had a dime for every time I have heard someone tell me that New York is a great place to visit but . . . when the real truth—for me, at least—is that the rest of the world may be a great place to visit, but New York is the place to live in.)

However, in flying over the eastern cities from Boston to

Washington, one is apt to get the feeling that there are no boundaries between states or cities or villages, that the whole 450-mile strip is one sprawling community, and that Megalopolis is really here. But there is a great deal more to the eastern, or Gateway, states than their coastal cities, and in these areas the lines of demarcation really become difficult. Where does the East leave off and the Midwest begin? Scratch a Minnesotan and he'll probably tell you Chicago. Ask a Philadelphian and he might say Buffalo. After all, wasn't Buffalo intended to be the beginning of the West? One major atlas defines the Middle West in part as being bounded by the Ohio River on the east. But the Ohio River starts at Pittsburgh, and is not Pennsylvania an eastern state? And where would you put West Virginia or Ohio?

Since the opening of the St. Lawrence Seaway to ocean shipping, even those bulwarks of the Midwest, Duluth and Chicago, are Gateway cities, and without stretching the imagination, they might be included in this Gateway to America section.

To add to the confusion, lying athwart this huge area is America's industrial heartland, which properly should be considered a region by itself. The geography may differ, but for practical comparisons the cities of Pittsburgh, Cleveland, and Detroit have much more in common with one another than with their own geographic neighbors. Born of industry, located on waterways, close to the resources of coal, iron, and chemicals that made them great, they have grown and prospered, and in so doing created a huge appetite for labor to man the forges, operate the rolling mills, and assemble the automobiles. Into this maw poured the millions, some of whom glanced briefly at the Statue of Liberty on their way west; some of whom never saw it at all, like the field hands from the Deep South or the dirt farmers from the Appalachians who pushed their way north over the rivers and trails.

All these people, once resettled, needed a roof over their heads, and for them houses were built, many hurriedly thrown together shoulder to shoulder on the hillsides and in the valleys around Pittsburgh and out on the flats around Cleveland and Detroit. And after the arrivals found work and a new way of life, many encouraged relatives or friends to come and live and work nearby, and so the ethnic enclaves were formed that ultimately rejected further entry by others.

From these beginnings the slums also grew, the buildings deteriorated, and the rot set in. With a growing middle class, the more affluent went scurrying to the suburbs in search of clean air, greenery, space, and perhaps a hoped-for, but rarely found, return to the peace of their earlier environments.

In their wake, the central areas of the great cities, first established because of their advantageous locations, fast became ugly, unappetizing neighborhoods and natural spawning places for crime and delinquency.

Of the three big cities in the industrial heartland, Pittsburgh probably was first to take a major step toward urban redevelopment. Just after World War II, planners constructed Gateway Center at the Golden Triangle, and transformed it from a blighted area into a gleaming complex of modern office buildings, new apartments, hotels, and theatres. In a second phase of development, the "new" Pittsburgh has extended far above the Golden Triangle, showing off a recently completed Civic Arena in addition to its latest group of apartments and office buildings. And a third area along the Allegheny River is now being readied for similar face-lifting.

To a lesser degree, there are signs of new growth in Cleveland and Detroit, but pitifully small so far, and the hard-core poverty areas smoldering in the heart of these urban centers ignited among the racial tinderboxes of 1967.

But interspersed between the major urban centers there are vast stretches of lovely farmland in mid-Pennsylvania, upper New York State, the heavily wooded Allegheny Mountains, and the backwater quiet of the inlets and reaches of the Chesapeake Bay area and the Eastern Shore of Maryland.

And in our nation's Capital, the big apartment blocks stretch farther and farther from downtown Washington out into

suburban Virginia and Maryland, even as an inward surge of the affluent snaps up the old buildings on the southeast and restores the once elegant town houses—turned slums—back into elegant town houses. If there ever was an aristocracy in America, what vestiges remain are comfortably dug in in Georgetown and the stately mansions along Massachusetts Avenue, though some have been replaced by the aristocracy of the Diplomatic Corps.

This reverse migration is quite apparent up and down the East Coast. The children of those post-World War II parents who fled to the suburbs have started leaving for college, and the fathers, wearying of catching the 7:23 from Greenwich, Harmon, Bala-Cynwyd, or other suburban enclaves, have started a full-blown stampede for the cities, swapping the lawn mower and hedge clipper for a terrace flower box with great glee. While this movement does not appear too distinct yet in the still great open spaces of this country, as the air-conditioned high-rise apartments rise still higher and spread still farther, the chilling thought does occasionally come through that someday this country may yet be paved from coast to coast or covered with a big plastic dome.

CENTRAL PARK, New York's 840-acre playpen, is in the heart of Manhattan, and over the years has served up a variety of treats for its citizenry. It is a place to cool off in the summer, ice-skate in the winter, ride a bike or a horse or even a statue of a horse, hear Shakespeare or a fine concert. It has everything that a great park should have, with a few features thrown in, such as an occasional mugging, a paint-in, a peace demonstration, and scooter-borne police who ride their snorting steeds as did the broncobusters of the Old West. Central Park is also a place to see lovers in the spring, take a hansom cab in the fall, feed the elephant in the zoo, or row a boat on its several lakes. Since its establishment, there have been countless suggestions to convert it to a residential area, a giant parking lot, or to lace it with expressways. Fortunately, all this "improvement" has been resisted, and New Yorkers have taken much pride in its preservation and increasing public use by all its people, whether young or old.

BORDERING CENTRAL PARK on the east, south, and west are some of the most elegant residences in the city. On the east, Fifth Avenue still contains many old town houses built by millionaires of generations back; Central Park South is edged by gracious hotels; and Central Park West is lined by big apartment houses, among them the old and stately Dakota Apartments (the building with the three sharply pitched gables) at the 72nd Street entrance to the Park, and now almost totally inhabited by many of New York's artistic and theatrical world and their families.

LOWER MANHATTAN AND BATTERY PARK separate the Hudson River (left) and the East River with its bridges to Brooklyn (upper right). The Customs House, Bowling Green, and the beginning of Broadway are to the right of the upper part of the park and on the edge of New York's financial center. Probably few native New Yorkers really know that the correct name for Battery Park is Castle Clinton National Monument. Originally constructed as a 19th-century fort, it became an opera house and then an immigrant receiving station where more then seven million new arrivals to America passed through from 1855 to 1890. Then it became New York City's Aquarium, was partially razed, and then restored as a monument.

12

THE EMPIRE STATE BUILDING (left), with its two observation levels, television transmitting tower, and lookout points commanding an 80-mile view on a clear day, has long been a landmark of New York; 102 stories high, it houses 16,000 office workers, and is the natural lure for almost every visitor coming to New York for the first time. The top of the tower is 1,472 feet above street level, and has been struck by birds, flying aircraft, and lightning. Construction of the building was finished in 1931, when it was thought that the tower could be used to moor transatlantic dirigibles, an idea not only impractical but impossible. The building is located at Fifth Avenue and 34th Street, the site of the old Waldorf-Astoria Hotel, now the southern end of the most popular shopping area in New York City.

EAST MIDTOWN MANHATTAN (above) is edged by the spired Chrysler Building, once second only to the Empire State Building as a landmark, but now outflanked by the massive Pan Am Building (left) with its own heliport. (Note helicopter landing on the roof pad.) Probably the biggest building in the city in terms of square footage, and considered by some to be the ugliest, it spawned immediate controversy the moment that plans were announced for its construction. Not only would thousands of office workers be dumped into an already overcrowded city center, but many voices of doom prophesied instant carnage as helicopters careened off the rooftop into the street below or impaled themselves on the Chrysler steeple. But for many travelers it provides the most spectacular view of the great city.

13

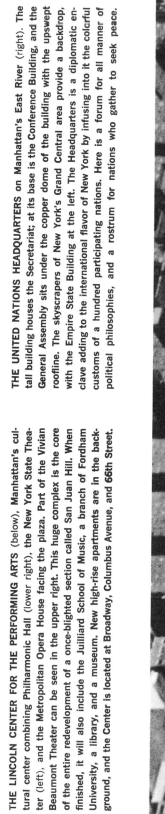

THE LINCOLN CENTER FOR THE PERFORMING ARTS (below), Manhattan's cultural center combining Philharmonic Hall (lower right), the New York State Theater (left), and the Metropolitan Opera House facing the plaza. Part of the Vivian Beaumont Theater can be seen in the upper right. This huge complex is the core of the entire redevelopment of a once-blighted section called San Juan Hill. When finished, it will also include the Juilliard School of Music, a branch of Fordham University, a library, and a museum. New high-rise apartments are in the background, and the Center is located at Broadway, Columbus Avenue, and 66th Street.

THE UNITED NATIONS HEADQUARTERS on Manhattan's East River (right). The tall building houses the Secretariat; at its base is the Conference Building, and the General Assembly sits under the copper dome of the building with the upswept roofline. The skyscrapers of New York's Grand Central area provide a backdrop, with the Empire State Building at the left. The Headquarters is a diplomatic enclave adding to the international flavor of New York by infusing into it the colorful customs of a hundred participating nations. Here is a forum for all manner of political philosophies, and a rostrum for nations who gather to seek peace.

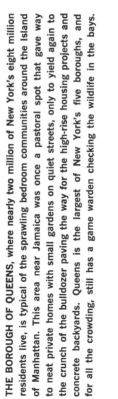

THE BOROUGH OF QUEENS, where nearly two million of New York's eight million residents live, is typical of the sprawling bedroom communities around the Island of Manhattan. This area near Jamaica was once a pastoral spot that gave way to neat private homes with small gardens on quiet streets, only to yield again to the crunch of the bulldozer paving the way for the high-rise housing projects and concrete backyards. Queens is the largest of New York's five boroughs, and for all the crowding, still has a game warden checking the wildlife in the bays.

THE VERRAZANO-NARROWS BRIDGE, soaring over the entrance to Upper Bay, is the longest single-span suspension bridge in the world. It also has what is probably the longest unused name as well, because typically most New Yorkers refer to it simply as the Narrows Bridge, and probably don't even know who Verrazano was. (Giovanni da Verrazano was an Italian navigator who discovered the entrance to New York's harbor in 1524.) Designed by famed bridgebuilder Othmar Hermann Ammann, who designed the nearby George Washington Bridge farther up the Hudson River, this graceful beauty has a center span of over 4,200 feet and an overall length of two and half miles connecting Brooklyn and Staten Island.

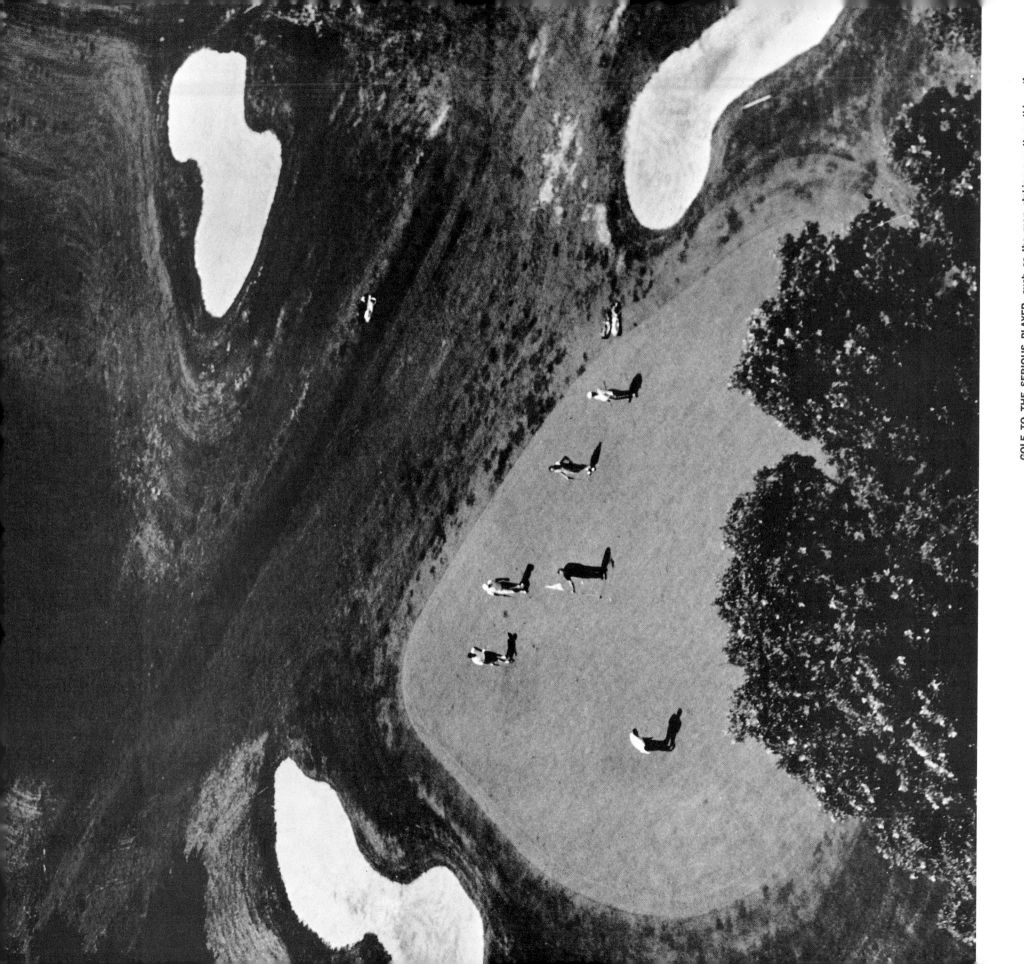

GOLF TO THE SERIOUS PLAYER, such as the man sinking a putt on this golf course out on Long Island, is so absorbing that he never even bothered to look up as my helicopter hovered almost directly overhead. Golf links, ball fields, racetracks, swimming pools, and country clubs have proliferated rapidly throughout the east as the rising population requires new areas of recreation and amusement. Unfortunately, too many country clubs are still socially segregated, and when an obliging pilot in the South pointed out one country club as belonging to a particular ethnic group, my only comment was, "That's funny, it really doesn't look it."

NEW YORK'S YANKEE STADIUM (below), long the home of the vaunted Bronx Bombers, has been the meeting place for everything from baseball and football games, soccer matches, rallies for Jehovah's Witnesses, Crusades by Billy Graham, and a temporary altar for Pope Paul during his historic one-day visit to New York. Its three-deck stands and bleachers can seat 67,000 people, and it has held more than 100,000 who have crowded into it on special occasions.

THE GARDEN STATE RACETRACK (above), near Camden, New Jersey, is another favorite gathering place for sports fans from New Jersey, nearby Philadelphia, and other Delaware River communities. The Garden State Races are held each Memorial Day, when the stands are jammed and the parking lots are chock-a-block with automobiles and buses. About the only ones with room to move are the horses, and any racegoer will tell you it's always the wrong horse at that.

FORT TICONDEROGA, in upper New York State, not only is steeped in history but also lies in one of the most beautiful settings in the East. The northern end of Lake George is separated from the southern end of Lake Champlain by Mount Defiance, a much-fought-over piece of real estate that was the ancient Indian portage between the two lakes and the gateway to the upper Hudson Valley from Canada. The fort itself was built in 1755 by the French, who called it Fort Carillon. In 1775 the Green Mountain Boys, commanded by Ethan Allen, captured it and sent its armament to Boston to relieve the siege by the British, who recaptured the fort in 1777.

THE MEGALOPOLIS CONCEPT of the eastern seaboard is demonstrated in this "fisheye" view of Newark, New Jersey (above), and its sprawling environs. From horizon to horizon, man's marks stretch every whichway. In this picture Jersey City is on the left horizon, with houses, schools, and factories pushing out in all directions as far as the eye can see. This urban crowding is not restricted to the New York metropolitan area, but spreads along a corridor 100 miles wide and 450 miles long, from Boston to Washington, D.C. This concentrated strip of less than 3% of the country's area holds nearly 20% of its total population.

THE PENN CENTER DEVELOPMENT sparkles as a counterpoint to the cleaned-up City Hall (above) and replaces what used to be called the Chinese Wall, a grim railroad right-of-way into the heart of downtown Philadelphia that effectively defied traffic and commerce. In its place is a multilevel complex of office buildings, shops, hotels, and a new Hospitality Center (the circular building in the shadow of City Hall). Nearer the Delaware River is an equally ambitious project restoring historic buildings and streets, eradicating slums, and building a modern residential neighborhood, which hasn't forgotten its past, within walking distance of the center.

PHILADELPHIA'S CITY HALL (left), with its statue of William Penn atop the lookout tower, has long been the butt of thousands of jokes about the school of architecture from which it derives. Called by some a classic example of Early Italian Contractor and by noted critic Lewis Mumford "an architectural nightmare," this baroque building stands in the very heart of the city, and, in spite of jibes, is much loved by Philadelphians and visitors alike. From the observation platform at the base of the statue, just under Penn's feet, one gets a sweeping panoramic view of what was once the largest city in the United States, and a vista that extends across the Delaware River to the east and up the Schuylkill River northwest.

THE ART MUSEUM (left) at the northwest end of the Benjamin Franklin Parkway is one of the finest art museums in America, with important collections of Far Eastern art, period rooms, and pre-Columbian pieces. It also includes a Chinese Buddhist temple, a medieval cloister, and many contemporary paintings.

SOUTH PHILADELPHIA'S face-lifting (right) manages to blend the old with the new. The Emanuel Lutheran Church at Fourth and Carpenter is preserved even as the terraced high-rise apartments surround it and the old gracious houses with their pleasant gardens and backyards disappear to be replaced by the architecture often called ice-cube modern.

INDEPENDENCE HALL (left), seat of the Second Continental Congress of the United States, and scene of the adoption of the Declaration of Independence, has been restored as a National Monument. The Liberty Bell hangs in the stairwell, and it was here the Constitution was first drafted. The buildings to the right are the old City Hall and the Philosophical Hall, both finished before 1791. The Mall is a recent addition to the restoration of the area by the State of Pennsylvania.

MARYLAND

THE QUIET REACHES OF CHESAPEAKE BAY are reflected in this serene farm on the bay's Eastern Shore. Chesapeake Bay drains the Susquehanna, Potomac, and James rivers, and is the source of prized oysters, blue crabs, and other seafood that makes eating a pleasure in so many fine restaurants found in the nearby cities. This historic area was first heavily populated by the Nanticoke, Wicomico, and Potomac Indians, then settled by the British, and much fought over during the American Revolution and the War of 1812. The bay extends for nearly 200 miles, with its navigable waterways reaching all the way from the Atlantic Ocean at Hampton Roads to the mouth of the Susquehanna River. Hundreds of creeks, coves, and inlets provide shelters and passage for the countless boats, ranging from the smallest punt used by a hunter in a duck blind to the ocean-spanning iron-ore carriers heading for Sparrows Point and the freighters, tankers, and other cargo carriers steaming up the Patapsco River into Baltimore Harbor.

THE SPARROWS POINT STEEL PLANT of the Bethlehem Steel Company is the largest of its kind in the world. A huge complex of blast furnaces, open hearths, coke ovens, and rolling mills, it sends much of its output to the adjacent shipyards that build ore carriers, freighters, and tankers. So much noise, smoke, and clatter pervade the scene that it would take a hardy sparrow indeed to roost there. Visitors seeing this vast area at night, with the skies lighted for miles around, are apt to think an entire city is aflame. It was the thrilling sight of fire at night, just a few miles away, at Fort McHenry protecting Baltimore's Harbor, that inspired Francis Scott Key to compose our National Anthem, "The Star-Spangled Banner." That time it was the unsuccessful attack by the British Navy on the night of September 13, 1814, that caused "the rocket's red glare, the bombs bursting in air," and one wonders to what creative heights Key might have risen had he ever seen the spectacular flaming nighttime skies around the Sparrows Point plant.

27

ANNE ARUNDEL'S TOWN, now called Annapolis, became the capital of Maryland in 1694, and has tried ever since to preserve its colonial heritage. The United States Naval Academy is located in this pretty town with its old brick walls and historic buildings. At the left is St. Anne's Church, first built in 1699 and then reconstructed in 1859. At the upper right is the State House, the oldest state capitol in continuous use since its construction in 1779. It was in the Old Senate Chamber that General George Washington resigned his commission as Commander in Chief of the Continental Army.

BALTIMORE'S INNER HARBOR (left) ranks fifth in tonnage in the United States, and actually is closer to the Midwest than any other Atlantic seaport. For this reason it is of prime importance as both railhead and terminus in the movement of grains, coal, and mineral ores. Deepwater shipping approaches from two directions: North Atlantic shipping coming through the Chesapeake and Delaware Canal and South Atlantic vessels moving through the Chesapeake Bay via Hampton Roads. The fine harbor itself is part of the estuary of the Patapsco River, and the docks on its 45-mile waterfront accommodate vessels up to 70,000 tons' displacement.

THE CITY OF BALTIMORE, like most major cities in the U.S., is undergoing a vast and much-needed modernization program. The heart of this new redevelopment is the Charles Center (above), providing a new exhibition hall, hotels, offices, and shops. But much of the past is still fondly preserved such as the old crenelated clock tower, simply known as the Bromo Seltzer Building, whose letters are used in place of the clock's numerals. Many of the old brick row houses still feature white stone steps, which are scrubbed regularly in an old civic tradition that is still scrupulously observed by many of Baltimore's proud homeowners.

WASHINGTON, D.C.

CAPITOL HILL is not dominated by the Capitol itself, as one might expect, but by the massive Rayburn Office Building (foreground), an $86-million mass of stone, steel, and congressional prerogatives that "Fortune" magazine called "A Monument to Power." Behind it are the other two House office buildings, then the Library of Congress and its Annex, the Supreme Court, and the two Senate office buildings. In the center is the Capitol on a site selected in 1791 by President George Washington and Major Pierre Charles L'Enfant, a French architect who fought in the American Revolution. L'Enfant planned the District of Columbia with broad boulevards, marble buildings, and beautiful fountains, all patterned after his beloved Paris. While much of his planning is still in evidence, there is also an abundance of government buildings whose style is often irreverently referred to as "General Service Gothic" or, in the case of the Rayburn Building, as "Texas Penitentiary" or even more simply as "Mr. Sam's Place."

THE WHITE HOUSE (left), facing on Pennsylvania Avenue, is the official residence of the President of the United States, and has been so used by every President except George Washington, who ordered it built. It was completed in 1799, shortly before Washington's death, and at that time only the central structure stood. The wings and terraces were added during President Jefferson's administration. It was burned by the British during the War of 1812 and restored by 1817; most succeeding Presidents added additional rooms, floors, porticoes, or columns until the whole building was declared unsafe during President Truman's occupancy. With only the outer walls left standing, the entire building was reconstructed and refurbished, the major acquisitions of historic furniture being collected by Mrs. Jacqueline Kennedy. To the right is the excessively ornate Executive Office Building, which once housed the State Department. The White House faces Lafayette Square; behind it are the Ellipse, Washington Monument, and the Jefferson Memorial.

THE LINCOLN MEMORIAL (above) on the banks of the Potomac is separated from the Washington Monument by the Reflecting Pond. Behind the Monument, the Mall stretches back toward the Capitol in keeping with L'Enfant's original plan for broad, sweeping vistas. The Lincoln Memorial, one of the more handsome structures in Washington, is girded by thirty-six Doric columns, one for each state in the Union at the time of Lincoln's death. In the main entrance is an impressive statue of Lincoln by the sculptor Daniel Chester French, with the Gettysburg Address inscribed on the stone tablets. The Washington Monument, a great stone obelisk of Maryland marble 555 feet high, is the tallest building in the District of Columbia, and is likely to remain that way in accordance with the zoning laws. An interior elevator and staircase lead to an observation room under the roof, giving the viewer a magnificent panoramic look at the city. Government office buildings seen here are the Navy Department on the left and the Bureau of Engraving on the right.

A FEW HOURS' DRIVE from the edges of Megalopolis are many lovely farms such as this one near Bedford in the fertile valleys of Pennsylvania. Here, interspersed between the industrial and mining towns, are calm backwaters of precisely tilled fields, carefully arranged stone walls, and well-pruned orchards that seem to ignore both the roar of trucks and cars speeding along the nearby Pennsylvania Turnpike and the nearby clatter of coal crashing down from the tipple into an endless line of gaping gondola cars.

PITTSBURGH

PITTSBURGH'S GOLDEN TRIANGLE (above) is at the confluence of the Allegheny and Monongahela rivers (left and right) where they form the Ohio River. The old Fort Pitt blockhouse, built as a frontier garrison in 1746, still holds its place in Point State Park, which has been reclaimed from a railroad freight terminal and an old slum. But the Golden Triangle, now brightened by the modern buildings of Gateway Center (background), was until World War II more a reflection of the old Pittsburgh, a grimy, smoky city whose air was so polluted by nearby steel plants that streetlights often burned twenty-four hours a day. In 1939, The Allegheny Conference on Community Development was formed because the situation had reached such life-choking proportions that even architect Frank Lloyd Wright's advice was "Abandon it!" Instead, Gateway Center was born, and a determined civic campaign got under way to secure the necessary legislation for slum clearance and pollution control, and soon the Smoky City no longer smoked.

PITTSBURGH'S CIVIC ARENA is part of the second phase of rebuilding the city. The first was Gateway Center, a 300-acre complex of new office buildings, shops, landscaped malls, and a hotel at the apex of the Triangle. Here, at the Triangle's base, the handsome domed stadium can be opened to the sky in a matter of minutes, and new offices and apartments are rising to reverse the flight to the suburbs. At one time this entire area was a slum called Lower Hill, and a few of those buildings can still be seen at the lower left. In the background is the central business district, which includes the new U.S. Steel and Alcoa buildings and the older Koppers and Gulf buildings. The area to the right, alongside the Allegheny River, is also slated for redevelopment and reclamation of its waterfront.

36

CLEVELAND

CLEVELAND'S NEW ERIEVIEW PLAZA TOWER and older Terminal Tower are symbolic of this eighth largest city in the United States, a vital steel, chemical, manufacturing and transportation center midway between New York and Chicago on Lake Erie. It is also a major cultural center, with excellent universities, an important orchestra, and fine art museum. Some of America's great fortunes were founded here too: John D. Rockefeller's Standard Oil Company and Mark A. Hanna's empire of coal, iron, and steel. But it was the Van Sweringen brothers, two colorful wheeler-dealers of their time, who played a major role in Cleveland's growth. Owning a vast tract of land in what is now Shaker Heights, they bought up the entire Nickel Plate Railroad just to acquire a short right-of-way to build a commuters' rapid-transit line. They also built the 52-story Terminal Tower complex in Public Square in the center of the city. Public Square also contains the Civil War Monument many consider among the ugliest of its kind in the United States.

CLEVELAND HEIGHTS (below), one of the residential communities that surround Cleveland, is a quiet area of middle-class housing, most of which contains pleasant front and back yards and enough trees to assure a suburban feeling. Actually, Cleveland Heights is one of several separate cities in the Greater Cleveland area, but, unlike Pittsburgh, the relatively flat terrain has given its inhabitants a chance to spread out. The Greater Cleveland area now houses nearly 2,000,000 people. It is an area of ethnic groups that tend to cluster in enclaves whose roots have grown from the vast number of Europeans who immigrated from Central Europe to work in the booming steel and auto plants but who still keep many of their Old Country traditions and tongues. It also has a large Negro population who, along with the white community, elected the first Negro mayor of a major city. Cleveland is also noted for its interracial Karamu House, a well-known art and theatre center that has contributed much to the city's cultural reputation.

THE CUYAHOGA RIVER VALLEY of Cleveland, known as "The Flats," is a major industrial center containing several steel mills, refineries, and chemical plants. It is also the major source of air and water pollution that fouls the streams and coats everything in the vicinity with a fine red patina of iron-ore dust. Through the narrow river thread the cumbersome Great Lakes steamers carrying their huge tonnages of coal, limestone, and iron ore, and from these mills and plants are shipped the vast quantities of iron, steel, and chemicals used widely around the world.

THE COAL DOCKS AT TOLEDO dominate this busy port in northwestern Ohio on Lake Erie. Coal from mines in Ohio, Kentucky, and West Virginia is brought in by rail, transshipped to Canada by lake steamer, or sent overseas by ocean freighter through the St. Lawrence Seaway. Iron ore is also received from the north.

DETROIT'S EXPRESSWAY SYSTEM befits the Motor City's automobile-based economy. Here the Edsel Ford Expressway intersects the John Lodge Expressway leading directly to the business section of the city on the Detroit River. Across the river is Windsor, Ontario, Canada's auto-manufacturing counterpart.

43

COBO HALL ON THE DETROIT RIVER is part of the Motor City's sparkling new $100-million Civic Center built on 75 acres of landscaped riverfront. One of the world's largest exhibition halls, and launching place for many new car models, it can seat some 14,000 people in the adjoining convention hall. A direct expressway connection to the circular ramp (left) leads to rooftop parking for 1,500 cars.

44

New England

WHAT ARE NOW THE STANDARD clichés about Yankee frugality, Puritanism, craftiness, and craftsmanship were simply statements of life in early New England. Here the colonists found an extraordinary setting of rocky coasts, sandy beaches, fine harbors, and coastal islands, backed by mountains, lakes, and dipping valleys. It was to be their "new" England—and they shaped the land to mirror their requirements for orderliness, cleanliness, and rugged self-dependence.

As the settlers arrived in increasing numbers from Europe, they created the maritime-oriented cities of Boston and Providence, and established the whaling and fishing ports along the coast from New Haven down to Eastport. After the fishermen came the farmers, loggers, and stone cutters who plunged inland to cultivate the valleys, bring out the timber, and open the great quarries. An abundance of water for power led to the establishment of factories that grew into the great textile centers, machine shops, toolmaking plants, and shipyards for which New England was noted.

But even as New England's economy grew and developed, the inevitable peak came and passed. As the nation prospered and expanded both west and south, the isolation of New England became as much a liability as an asset.

Once the pride of New England, the rivers and streams became polluted by chemicals and waste, the forests depleted by textile and paper industries, and the cities and towns, especially those dependent on the older industries, began to wither. Factories closed and moved south. The fishing fleets, long a bulwark of the economy, began to suffer. The famous Grand Banks, once primarily the domain of New England and Canadian fishermen, suddenly burgeoned with ships of all registries, many operating at cost factors far below those with which New Englanders could reasonably compete. For a time the future of New England looked as bleak as some of its rocky farms and rugged coast.

But New England's saving grace also had its origin back in Puritan times, for the settlers who founded the colonies also founded schools that later grew into some of the greatest centers of learning of our nation. And now this early investment in culture and education began to pay off. The new electronics industries, which require more brains than floor space, began to seek accessibility to the great technical and educational centers, particularly in the Boston area, but spreading elsewhere too, throughout New England.

Starting just after World War II, schools such as MIT, Harvard, Tufts, Brown, and Dartmouth suddenly became the

happy hunting grounds for industrial recruiters representing everything from flypaper to flight plans.

Boston and adjoining Cambridge, as well as other nearby communities, are no longer places that happen to contain schools —they are acknowledged as *the* gathering places for young intellectuals; and though Boston is one of the oldest cities in the nation, we find it considered one of the youngest. New architecture has revitalized the once-decaying city center, and the Back Bay has turned into a beehive of reconstruction and refurbishing of historic old houses.

New England with its mountains, lakes, and beaches has always been a haven for the summer vacationer, be he a youngster in a summer camp with a pseudo-Indian name, a tycoon in his forty-room "cottage" at Newport, a newspaperman lolling on the beach at Menemsha Bight on Martha's Vineyard, or just one of the many thousands who regularly dash to and from Cape Ann, Cape Cod, or Portsmouth in a bumper-to-bumper death dance each Friday and Sunday evening in the summertime. Time was when this madness was confined to the summer vacation months, but the fall hunting season, and increasing popularity of the ski slopes of Vermont, New Hampshire, and Massachusetts have made the northeast more of a year-round vacation place. The investment in ski towns, lodges, and inns for the winter vacationer grows enormously each year to the point that a resident is just as likely to be impaled by a pair of ski poles in the winter as he was in danger of being mistaken for a deer in the fall or run down by an outboard in the summer.

But with all the changes, growth, and redevelopment, the spirit of New England remains curiously unchanged. Away from the city centers, covered bridges are not only preserved and repaired but also rebuilt with great loving care. The old churches are carefully painted and kept up, and the new ones are built in the traditional style, as if they were almost embarrassed to be new.

The big barns in Vermont appear to last forever in spite of the ravages of time and forays of the modern interior decorators who scour the countryside looking for weatherbeaten boards to panel a rumpus room or a bar. At Menemsha, the old swordfishing fleet has survived, for the most part, the disastrous hurricanes of years back. And if it's a shock to walk along the pier at night and see the cabins illuminated by TV screens rather than kerosene lamps, it's most reassuring to see the traditional rigging silhouetted against the sky, and know this hardy strain of New Englanders not only survives with a lusty vigor but is more productive than ever before in their long and often colorful past.

AN OLD COVERED BRIDGE in northern Vermont is typical of many of these historic structures still in service in New England.

BOSTON

THE STATE HOUSE FACING BOSTON COMMON in the heart of the city has not changed too much since it was built in 1798. The State House faces Beacon Street. Tremont Street is on the right, and Park Street connects the two. At the intersection of Park and Tremont is the Park Street Church, built in 1809. Behind it is the Granary Burying Ground, final resting-place of Paul Revere, John Hancock, Samuel Adams, and other prominent patriots of their time.

THE PRUDENTIAL CENTER (left) looms over the Christian Science Mother Church in the fashionable Back Bay. The 52-story tower is part of a spirited urban renewal program to revitalize a decaying section of historic Boston. Behind the tower is the Charles River over which Paul Revere rowed to begin his famous ride. On the far side are eminent Harvard College, Radcliffe College, and the renowned Massachusetts Institute of Technology.

THE NORTH END OF BOSTON (right), location of the Old North Church (lower right) where the signal lanterns were hung to start Paul Revere on his historic ride in April, 1775, is overshadowed by the new Government Center rising in the background. If Paul Revere had to repeat his journey today, he would be well advised to keep his horse, because traffic congestion in the Boston area is such that a car might not make it in equal time. At the upper left, near the tall building under construction, is historic Faneuil Hall, scene of many a town meeting during the crucial revolutionary days and often called the Cradle of Liberty.

49

50

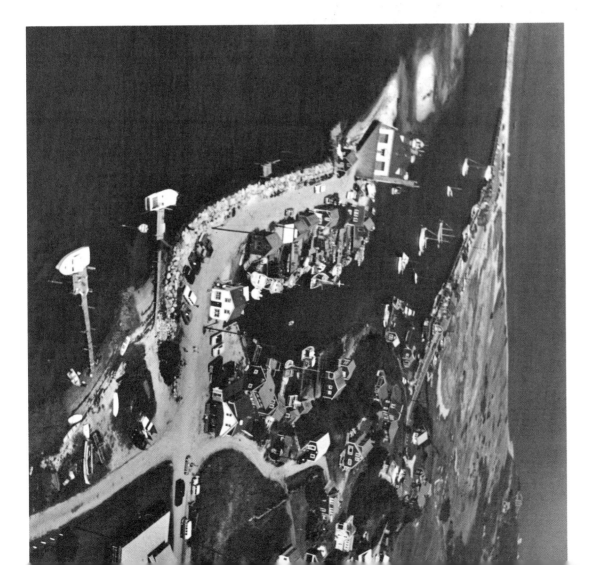

HARVARD UNIVERSITY IN CAMBRIDGE (left), across the Charles River, was founded in 1636, and is the oldest college in the United States. In addition to teaching thirty-three undergraduate fields, it has ten professional schools with many graduate, scientific, and research centers. Harvard Square is at right, and the Widener Library is upper center, facing Harvard Yard and some of the dormitories.

THE SNUG HARBOR AT MENEMSHA BIGHT on Martha's Vineyard Island off Cape Cod has long been a haven for swordfishermen, yachtsmen, and some seafarers who have never managed more than a rowboat. It is a favorite vacation place for those preferring quiet beaches and atmosphere undisturbed by the strenuous planning of hotel social directors, of which there are none on this charming island.

RHODE ISLAND

PROVIDENCE, RHODE ISLAND (above), was, from its establishment in 1636, a haven for nonconformists. Its founder, Roger Williams, welcomed Baptists, Jews, and Quakers, got along with the Indians, who gave him extensive land grants, and established a prosperous city that still retains many of its earlier traditions. Brown University (above) overlooks the city, and the state Capitol is upper right.

CLIFF WALK AND BAILEY'S BEACH at Newport have shown off the summer "cottages" of America's wealthy and socialite world since 1870. Many of the fine old mansions were built before the turn of the century as summer havens for such famous names as Vanderbilt, Astor, Thaw, Belmont, Bryce, and others. While many rich elite families still summer here, death, taxes, and the lack of servants have all taken their toll; and "The Waves," the great house in the foreground on Ledge Road, originally built by noted Newport architect John Russell Pope for himself, has been converted into an apartment house, as have other showplaces.

THE PIERS AT NEWPORT are still the moorages for many large boats, though the days of the old steam yachts that could cross the ocean and needed crews of fifteen or twenty are gone. But the sailing spirit is still strong and kept active by the hosting of the International America's Cup Race and other regattas that are surrounded by socially important events and attract sportsmen of all nations.

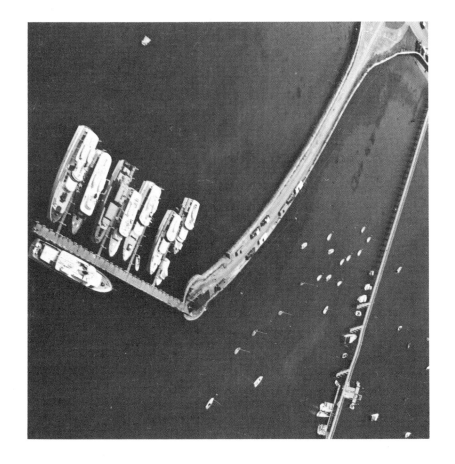

FORTITUDE IN VERMONT is not restricted to winters on the farms and villages. A new strain of American hardiness has enabled city folks to spend hours at the ski slopes waiting for the chair lifts and T-bars that carry them to the tops of the mountains. In fact, a whole new type of skier has evolved. He is called the non-skier, and spends most of his or her time in the base lodges, such as this one at the foot of Spruce Mountain near Stowe, avoiding the slopes like the plague, but all the time avidly watching for non-skiers of the opposite sex to non-ski with.

VERMONT IN THE WINTER still requires farmers to have much of the personal fortitude that characterized the early New England settlers. This farm (left) just north of Stowe has the big barns and outbuildings that must protect an entire herd of cattle and large flocks of poultry through savage winters with temperatures often plummeting to twenty degrees below zero. While most farms are equipped with modern amenities, life on them is still a rigorous existence requiring a never-ending battle with a rugged terrain and often hostile elements.

NEW HAMPSHIRE

NEW HAMPSHIRE WITH ITS LOVELY VILLAGES, lakes, and forested mountains is not unlike Vermont except for its outlet to the sea, a narrow neck between Massachusetts and Maine near Portsmouth. The villages, such as this one about thirty miles north of Concord, are built traditionally around a common, with colonial churches dominating the architecture. Just as the winters are cold and hard, so are the summers cool and soft, and the mountains and beaches are much sought after as vacation spots for beleaguered urbanites seeking escape from the heat.

RYE BEACH NEAR PORTSMOUTH is New Hampshire's sun-and-sand strip on the Atlantic Ocean, and, like the Vermont non-skiers, the cold Atlantic seems to have produced a breed of non-swimmers who understandably prefer to lie on the sand soaking up sun and musing about the hardiness of those brave enough to go in.

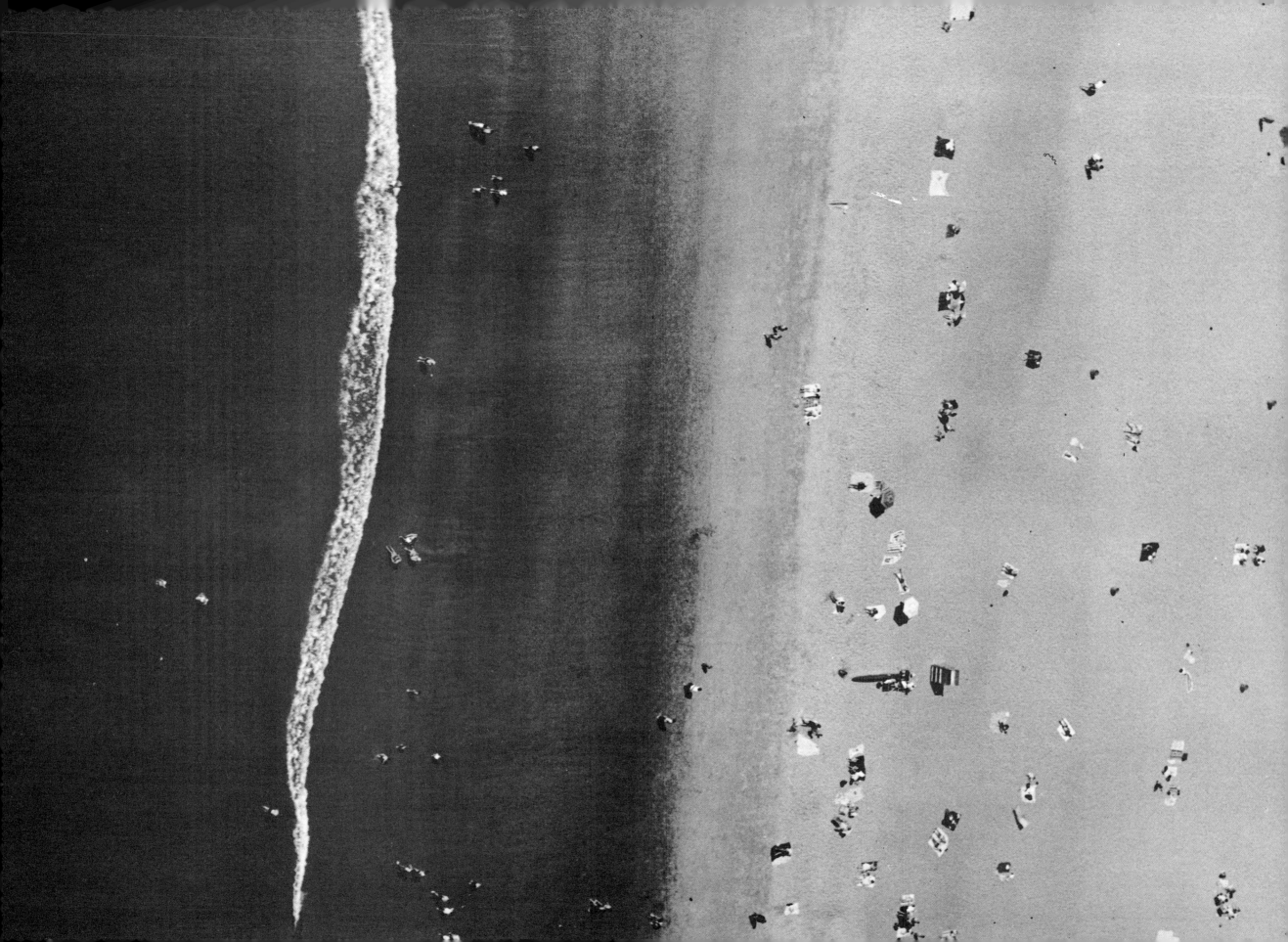

THE ROCKY COAST OF MAINE near Eastport is just about as far "down East" as one can go. From these cold waters come the prized Maine lobsters, and at Eastport is the Bay of Fundy whose enormous tidal drop has long fascinated engineers with its promise of cheap electric power. Construction of the Passamaquoddy Tidal Power Project was actually begun under President Roosevelt, but immediately ridiculed by newspapermen, who had great fun printing cartoons of Indians shooting the insulators of the electric-light poles with bows and arrows. The project was killed by Republican opposition in Congress at the onset of World War II. However, Maine's continued need for electric power has twice prompted her Republican senators to ask the Corps of Engineers for new feasibility studies, but each time the cost projections proved to be too high, and the idea died. Moreover with atomic power available, it is likely that Quoddy will stay buried.

The Midwest

THOUGH THERE IS INDEED a Midwest in this country, some question does persist as to where to draw its western boundaries. In trying to fix this dividing line, I have asked a number of people who were, presumably, Midwesterners, and their answers were no less amusing than they were confusing.

One bright-eyed girl from northern Michigan steadfastly asserted that the Midwest had to be restricted, naturally, to those states which had Big Ten football teams. When I asked her about Kansas and the Dakotas, she threw up her hands in horror and said, "Oh, those are the Plains States, not part of the Midwest at all." But a South Dakota wheat farmer told me he considered (and I tend to agree with him) that the Midwest ends at the eastern slope of the Rocky Mountains.

Whatever the actual boundaries, the generalizations that most people make about the Midwest are more or less correct. The land is mostly flat and fertile, serving not only as the nation's breadbasket but also as the storehouse for much of the world's grain. Yet apart from the level acres of farms, there is great variety to the Midwest in landscape, from the timbered lakes of northern Wisconsin, Michigan, and Minnesota to the cornbelt of Illinois and Indiana, which also are centers of industry in steel, auto and farm machinery plants.

The Midwest is an area blessed not only with lush crops and busy cities but also with mineral resources. The northern regions are veined with iron ore and limestone; and though the high-grade Mesabi ores are diminishing, the pelletizing process has brought a new life to the iron-ore industry by making the vast deposits of secondary ores economical to mine. The region from Ohio to the Dakotas is dotted with oil fields, and in the south, extensive deposits of lead, silver, zinc, and coal all contribute extensively to the nation's mineral wealth.

The population of the Midwest tends to be drawn to the eastern urbanized sections, but the cities are generally small, and rarely is it more than a few minutes' drive from Main Street of any midwestern center to the apron of a flourishing farm area.

The waterways of the Midwest are great and numerous, and while the Mississippi River frequently evokes thoughts of the South, it starts here in northern Minnesota. The Missouri, Ohio, Wabash, Cumberland, Platte, Red, Arkansas, and Canadian rivers and their tributaries drain the great mountain chains to the east and west. And it is commonplace to see the big river towboats shoving 1,200-foot bargeloads of grain, oil, steel, chemicals, or finished automobiles.

Yet for all the work of man, the floods and violence of the great rivers are still to be reckoned with. The Corps of Engineers has spent a lifetime and billions of dollars in straightening river

bends and building dams and levees to contain the mighty rush of water released each year by the melting snows.

A huge lore of literature has sprung up about life on the rivers, of which Mark Twain's tales are probably the most famous, though only a small part of the legacy. Most of the paddle-wheel coal-burning packet boats are gone now, though in the upper Ohio a few doughty old stern-wheelers are still pushing barges of coal. And gone to a well-deserved rest in the river museum in Vicksburg is the mighty old Sprague, more affectionately known as "Big Mama," the greatest towboat ever built: 314 feet long, 61 feet wide, with a huge stern paddle wheel. Her steam whistle in full throat calling for fish from a johnboat could be heard for miles on each side of the river, and her galley crew of eight often served ten different kinds of pie for breakfast.

In place of "Big Mama" is a whole new generation of river Goliaths such as the Mississippi Valley Barge Line's Lillian Clark, generating 6,000 horsepower, equipped with radar, Fathometers, and marine telephones for all-weather navigation, in addition to such amenities for the crew as TV, air conditioning, and private cabins. Today, big towboats like the Lillian Clark rarely stop once a tow is made up and under way. Fuel and provisions are transferred in midstream by river-going tankers, and even though the shoreline is but a few hundred feet away, most crew members never set foot on it from a trip's beginning to end.

The climate of the Midwest can best be described as rigorous, with extremes in both winter and summer. In winter, temperatures of 40 and 50 degrees below zero are not uncommon in northern Minnesota, while in the summer the searing sun sends the thermometers well over 100 degrees in the shade . . . and in most places there is not much shade. The winter snows pile up and isolate communities by the thousands, yet the inhabitants seem to take all this with a sort of stoic pride. A few years back, one farmer told me that hail had destroyed nearly 80 percent of his wheat crop just a few days before the harvest, and had it not been for the government crop insurance, his family would have been hard pressed to get through the year. Typically, though, he looked ahead to the following year, confident that his lands would yield more than fifty bushels per acre.

Once I came to Minneapolis unexpectedly, just after a severe winter storm had dropped twenty inches of snow on it and plummeted the temperature to 31 degrees below zero. Yet the streets were open, the cars moved easily, and people came to and from work without much comment about the severity of the weather. If half of this had happened in New York, the city would have been paralyzed and the weather would have remained a conversation piece for five years to come or longer.

THE OHIO RIVER AT EVANSVILLE, Indiana, makes a great double bend before continuing its meandering route to join with the Mississippi River at Cairo, Illinois. One of America's great waterways, the Ohio is navigable for its full 981 miles from Cairo to Pittsburgh. The Corps of Engineers maintains a minimum channel of nine feet to accommodate the huge towboats and barges. The Corps also strives to contain the ever-wandering river within its banks because the boundary lines of the six states on the Ohio are determined by the low-water mark on the north bank of the river rather than by the river itself. Gone is the gauger who took hand soundings of the river's depth, and sang them to the pilothouse—now replaced by a fathometer that will never cry out "Mark Twain" at twelve feet of water. And radar has eliminated the tie-ups at the riverbanks waiting for the fog to lift.

60

OHIO RIVER

A WHOLE NEW GENERATION of river towboats, such as the 6,000-horsepower Lillian Clark (right), now plies the rivers. Equipped with radar, telephones, and fathometers, even the megaphone used by the deckhands to talk to the shore has been replaced by the electronic bullhorn. But what the old river buffs probably miss the most is the black smoke pouring from the stacks of the old stern-wheelers and the singsong litany of the gaugers sounding the water's depth. The Mississippi with its errant channels and sandbars had to be sounded more frequently than the lock-controlled Ohio, but the calls were the same: Quarter Less Twain (10½ ft.); Quarter Twain (13½ ft.); Quarter Less Tyree (16½ ft.); Quarter Tyree (19½ ft.); Quarter Less Four (22½ ft.); Mark Twain (12 ft.); Half Twain (15 ft.); Half Tyree (21 ft.); Mark Four (24 ft.).

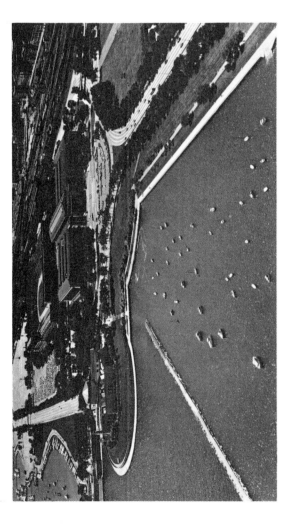

CHICAGO

THE MARINA IN CHICAGO HARBOR on Lake Michigan provides a quiet backwater away from the roaring Loop. Behind it is the Natural History Museum (or the Field Museum), named after Marshall Field; behind that is Soldier Field (no relation to Marshall Field), seating 100,000 people.

THE CHICAGO RIVER, a navigable stream connecting the Great Lakes with the Mississippi River, curls through the city at the north end of the Loop. Flanking the river on the north side is the twin-towered Marina City apartment house, the most spectacular in Chicago. On both sides of the river are office buildings and hotels, some new, such as the United Insurance Company building opposite Marina City, and some old, like the classic Wrigley Building, the white structure with the tower at the river curve.

GRANT PARK AND BUCKINGHAM FOUNTAIN are in Chicago's front yard between Michigan Avenue and Lake Michigan. This 303-acre greensward contains beautiful flower beds, the illuminated Memorial Fountain, a band shell for public concerts in the summer, and the famous Chicago Institute.

MADISON, WISCONSIN

THE STATE CAPITOL OF WISCONSIN at Madison is unusual because of the four identical wings spreading from the huge central dome. Located on a narrow isthmus between lakes Mendota and Monona, this pleasant Midwestern city is not only the state capital but also the seat of the main campus of the University of Wisconsin.

THE UNIVERSITY OF WISCONSIN campus refutes the joke about a Big Ten College being a small group of buildings next to a large football stadium. While the stadium may qualify, the 6,000 students at this campus (more than 20,000 in all branches) feel that this self-contained city is quite big enough, thank you.

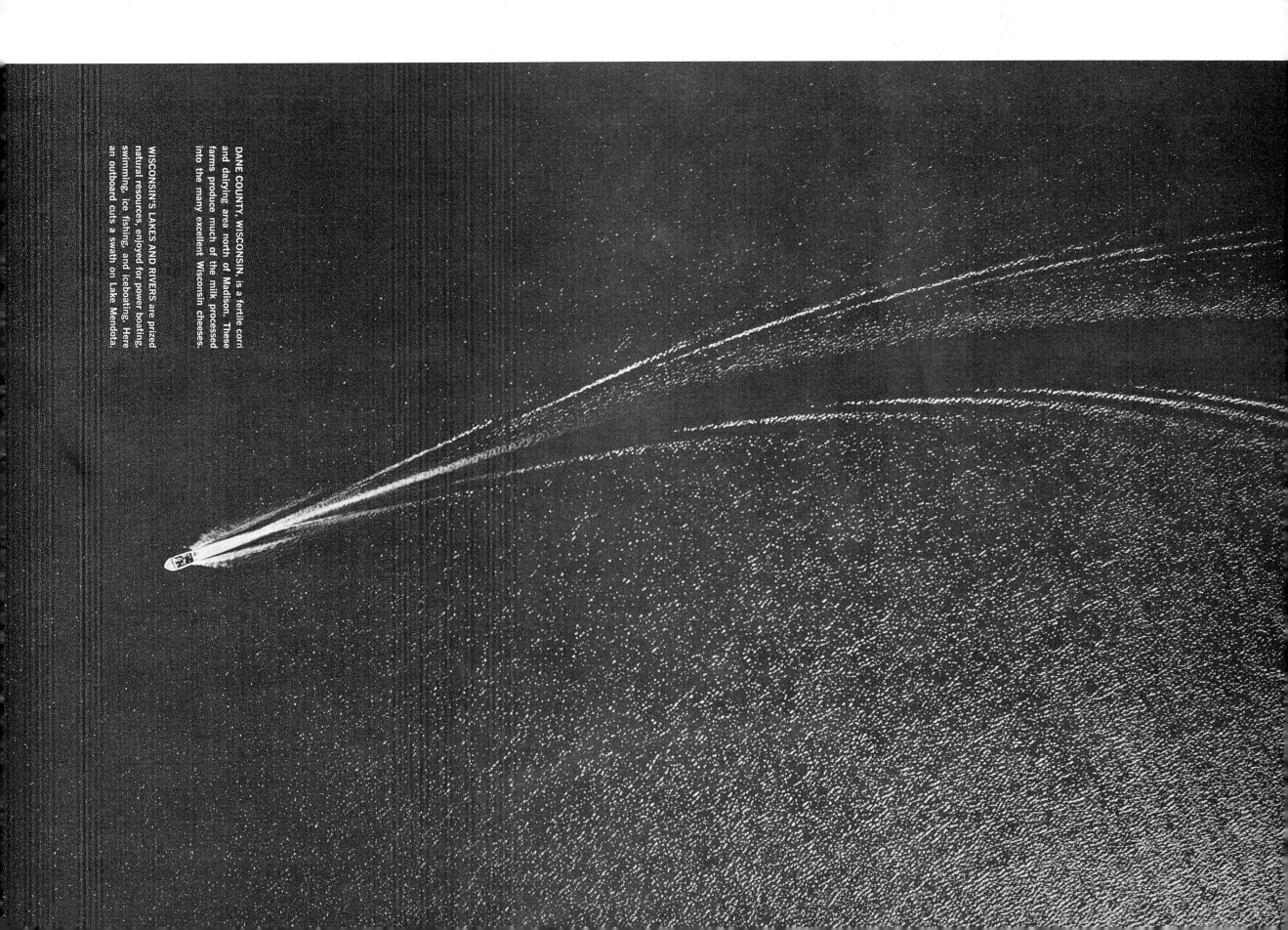

DANE COUNTY, WISCONSIN, is a fertile corn and dairying area north of Madison. These farms produce much of the milk processed into the many excellent Wisconsin cheeses.

WISCONSIN'S LAKES AND RIVERS are prized natural resources, enjoyed for power boating, swimming, ice fishing, and iceboating. Here an outboard cuts a swath on Lake Mendota.

MINNESOTA

THE TWIN CITIES of Minneapolis and St. Paul together form a metropolitan district ranking 10th in area and 14th in population in the U.S. Minneapolis is a vast flour-milling, manufacturing, and educational center, and the largest city in the state. It is the home of the University of Minnesota, a number of smaller colleges, the famous Minneapolis Symphony Orchestra, three excellent art galleries, and the nationally known Tyrone Guthrie Repertory Theater.

THE CITY OF ST. PAUL, like Minneapolis, fronts on the Mississippi River, and is fast catching up to its sister city as a flour-milling, manufacturing, and distribution center for the North Central states. It is the state capital, and boasts the handsome St. Paul Cathedral, as well as several important theological institutions. At the junction of the Mississippi and Minnesota rivers on the southern edge of the city is Fort Snelling State Park, built around the historic fort.

69

DULUTH, MINNESOTA, at the head of Lake Superior, coexists with Superior, Wisconsin, in providing a shipping point for much of the nation's iron ore and grain, as well as a receiving terminal for Canadian oil, wheat, and timber. Here an iron-ore carrier passes under the Aerial Lift Bridge before entering Lake Superior, en route to the steel-making centers of Detroit, Pittsburgh, and Cleveland.

SUPERIOR, WISCONSIN, twin port of Duluth, is studded with gigantic grain elevators that handle huge tonnages of American and Canadian wheat, as well as shiploads of other farm products. Both harbors are formed by the mouth of the St. Louis River, and are protected from Lake Superior by two sandbars, named, aptly enough, Minnesota Point and Wisconsin Point, each pierced by a ship canal.

71

THE IRON-ORE DOCKS at Superior are in keeping with the Bunyanesque concepts of the North Central states. Each of these gigantic docks can accommodate up to four iron-ore carriers on each side simultaneously, and the four parallel tracks on the top can handle 100 car trains apiece to maintain a steady flow of ore into the waiting holds of the freighters.

MINNESOTA'S NICKNAME, the "Land of 10,-000 Lakes," is really an understatement, because there are actually more than 13,000 of them, plus uncounted ponds, streams, and creeks, all of which add up to a scenic lure for fishermen, hunters, and campers. This series of lakes between Brainerd and Bemidji is typical of an area abounding in fish and wildlife. And nestled at the shores are the summer places that are the retreats of the urbanites.

THE MISSISSIPPI RIVER near its headwaters at Lake Itasca in northwestern Minnesota winds and twists in a mini-version of itself in southern Louisiana 2,300 miles away. By the time Big Muddy has reached its delta in the Gulf of Mexico, it has carried with it some 400 million tons of rich bottom soil each year, and has increased the size of the delta area by a full mile every 15 or 16 years. However, the new land is totally inaccessible.

PAUL BUNYAN AND BABE the Blue Ox are immortalized by 18-foot statues in the main street of Bemidji (above), a logging town in northern Minnesota also noted for its ferocious winters. Paul, a legendary lumberjack of superhuman strength, and his assistant, Babe, are credited with felling entire forests in a day, shifting and straightening river bends, scooping out the Great Lakes, and ultimately digging out Puget Sound to bury Babe.

ARKANSAS' ALUMINUM INDUSTRY is centered near Hurricane Creek, southwest of Little Rock, where substantial bauxite deposits sparked the development of the aluminum industry in the state. These drying kilns of the Reynolds Metals Company are part of the complex operations to convert the bauxite into aluminum.

BAUXITE FROM A STRIP MINE is the basic ingredient of aluminum. Here a scraper loosens the hard crust of the bauxite ore, which is then loaded into trucks and taken to the nearby processing plant. The bauxite will be refined into alumina, which is reduced electrically in a potline and converted into aluminum ingots.

SOUTH DAKOTA

THE BIG WHEAT SPREADS of South Dakota reach to the limitless horizons as the big combines follow the wheat harvest on the move from Texas to Canada. During the height of the harvest season it is not unusual to see a motorcade of twenty combines, some of them air-conditioned (as is the one in the small picture), and their supporting cars and trucks traveling along the highway like an army on the march. Because their services are used only once a year and the equipment is both expensive and complicated, few farmers own their own combine equipment, preferring to hire contract combiners to harvest their crops. Speed and efficiency are the watchwords, because a sudden storm can undo a year's work, and the farmer who cultivates hundreds and, in some cases, thousands of acres of wheat needs to have his crop brought in swiftly and safely.

THE BADLANDS OF SOUTH DAKOTA, in the southwestern part of the state, cover nearly 2,000 miles of wind-eroded buttes, pinnacles, and fluted ridges. The many-hued cliffs, formed by flash floods and strong winds, are mostly barren of vegetation, though in some of the lower gullies there is enough grass for a few cattle. The constant erosion has uncovered fossils estimated to be thousands of years old.

MOUNT RUSHMORE NATIONAL MONUMENT, in the Black Hills of South Dakota, is adorned with the gargantuan sculptures of four presidents of the United States: Washington, Jefferson, Theodore Roosevelt, and Lincoln. Authorized by Congress in 1925, sculptor Gutzon Borglum was commissioned to design the memorial. He died in 1941, before it was finished, and his son Lincoln completed the work.

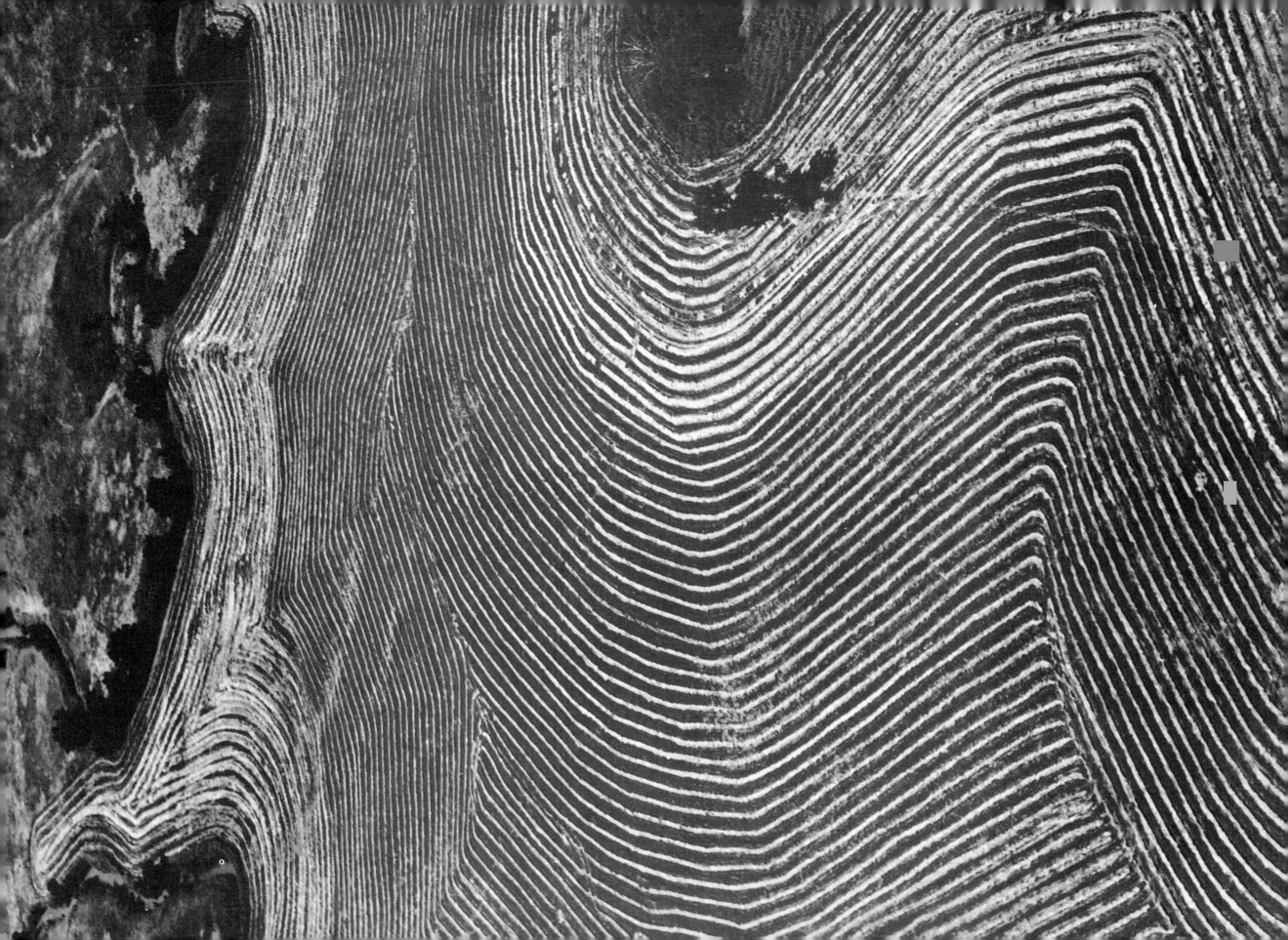

ST. LOUIS

THE GATEWAY ARCH in St. Louis towers 630 feet above a mall. This beautiful stainless-steel structure, designed by the late Eero Saarinen as part of the Jefferson National Expansion Memorial, commemorates the westward expansion of the United States in which St. Louis played an historic part. Inside the arch, small capsules carry passengers aloft for a sweeping view of the city.

A SMALL FARM IN THE BLACK HILLS of South Dakota. Because of the stony terrain in western South Dakota, farmers plant where they can, and this small parcel is carefully wedged in the rich bottomland between two massive stone hills to take advantage of the natural irrigation of snow and rain runoff.

ST. LOUIS LOVES ITS RIVER and has preserved much of the steamboat flavor of the Mississippi. Old packet boats are converted into floating restaurants, gas lights illuminate some of the city's streets, and beer is an item not only manufactured and exported but also consumed locally in great quantities. A major manufacturing city, it produces aircraft, automobiles, spacecraft, riverboats, and railroad cars, and more than two million people now live and work here.

KANSAS CITY, MISSOURI, the second largest city in the state, has modernized with a new building program boasting of several new hotels, office buildings, and a network of expressways. The suburbs, too, have exploded with high-rise apartments, an expanded park system, and broad shopping centers. All this is a far cry from the two frontier settlements that formed the original city back in the 1830's and 1840's, when westward-bound settlers debarked from Missouri River steamers to begin their trek over the Oregon and Santa Fe trails. With the coming of the railroads, Kansas City took a dominant position in grains and cattle.

84

BROAD AND MEETING STREETS IN CHARLESTON, South Carolina, are marked by four historic buildings that have graced this early-American city almost since it was first founded. St. Michael's Episcopal Church is in the center, and clockwise are the Post Office, the County Court House, and the City Hall erected in 1801.

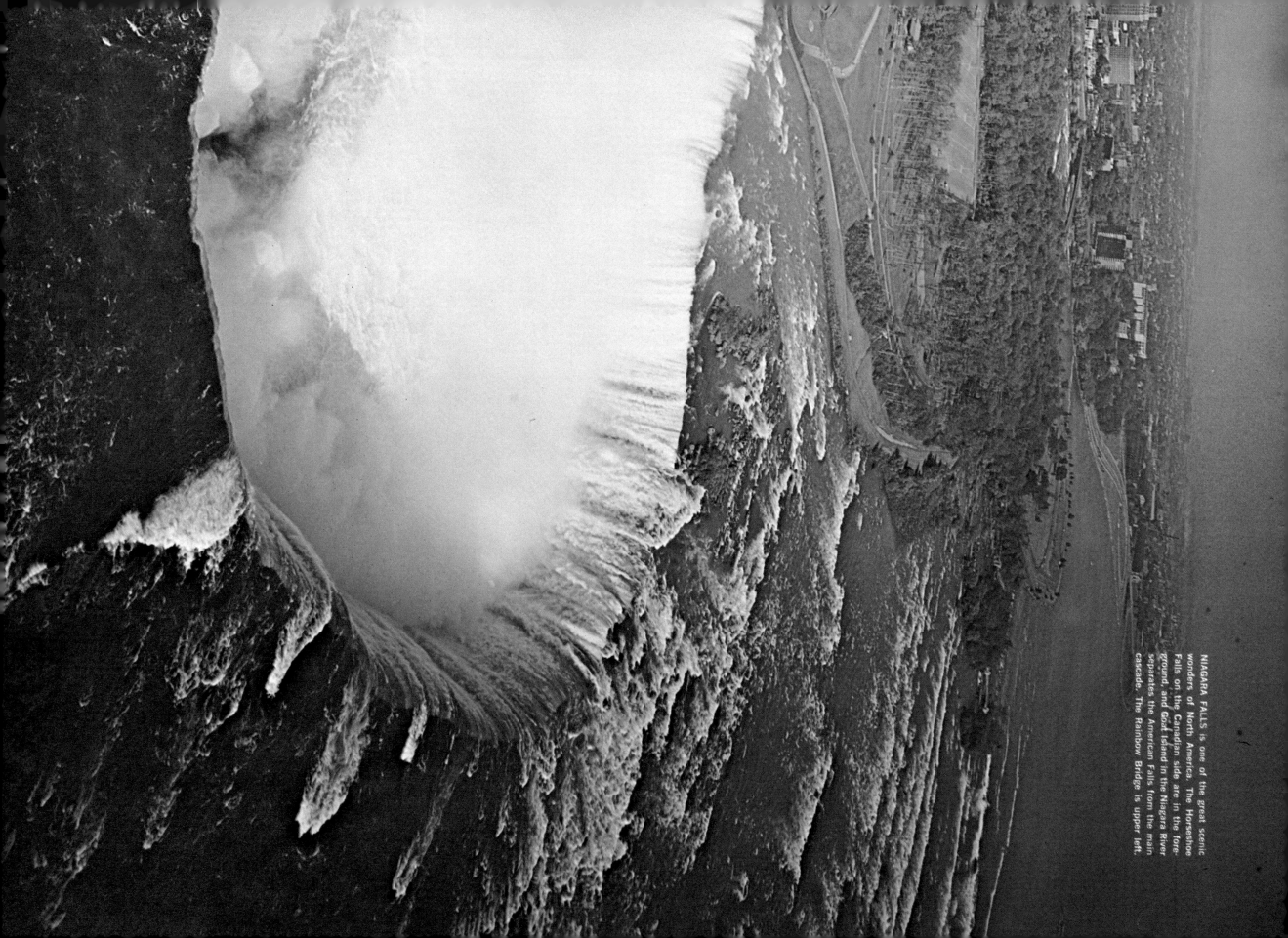

NIAGARA FALLS is one of the great scenic wonders of North America. The Horseshoe Falls on the Canadian side are in the fore- ground, and Goat Island in the Niagara River separates the American Falls from the main cascade. The Rainbow Bridge is upper left.

VACATIONING, PLAYING, and sight-seeing are America's favorite forms of recreation and they are symbolized by the ornate motel in North Miami Beach (above), the huge pool at Bear Mountain Park with the bathers in the water or sunbathing on the green, and, of course, the Statue of Liberty standing on a small island in New York City's Upper Bay.

RURAL AMERICA keeps its classic beauty of well-tended farms and orderly villages to serve the agricultural communities around them. The snow-covered farm at the left is just north of Stowe in Vermont, and the village above is Dane, Wisconsin, near Madison. The church and its tiny graveyard, the firehouse in the upper right, and the farm implement dealer in the lower right all blend together into one self-sufficient village and social center for the farmers.

THE BELCHING SMOKESTACKS of the huge furnaces of the Great Lakes Steel Company plant pour tons of pollutants into the sky south of Detroit. All it needs is a strong wind to carry it upstream to the Motor City, which is probably used to it, or across the river into Canada, which literally must take a dim view of this form of free enterprise that leaves a coat of red iron-ore dust on all it touches.

The Southeast

AS ONE PROCEEDS down the Atlantic Coast to the tip of Florida, it's all too easy to lump everything below Washington, D.C., as the "South," and shrug one's shoulders. But the southeastern coastal areas have an individuality quite apart from the "Deep South" of Alabama, Mississippi, and western Georgia.

With the sea at their doorstep, Norfolk, Savannah, and Charleston were all commercial ports from the start, heavily influenced by the European traders and immigrants who streamed through the harbors and settled down on the flat, open savannas.

Starting in the early 1600's—and for the next two hundred years—the port cities were also the slave-trading centers, and the economic prosperity fostered a style of living that soon gave rise to the stereotypes of southern graciousness, charm, hospitality, and perhaps southern indolence.

The "southern" way of life also took its cue from the climate and resources. The coastal lands were hot, humid, and swampy, so those who stayed built houses with balconies and galleries to enjoy the evening breezes, and the rooms were high-ceilinged to avoid the heat. The forests, rich in pine and cypress, became the core of the naval stores' industry that supplied busy shipyards with timber and pitch. Eli Whitney's invention of the cotton gin in 1793, and the abundance of waterpower and slave labor, quickly established cotton as the prime crop. And the railroad age was born with the first steam railroad operating between Charleston and Atlanta in the 1830's.

Though it began steadily, this rapid growth ended abruptly in 1860 with the outbreak of the Civil War. Five years of savage and destructive warfare, subsequent plagues of boll weevils, and all the attempts to revert to the prewar days of life took their respective tolls, and the South's wheels became mired as if they were axle-deep in the ever-present red clay. The emancipated slaves began to compete for work, to be pushed back by the pattern of segregation that had its real roots in the economic competition for jobs. The vicious results made the whole nation suffer, but the South suffered most as vast numbers of Negroes and poor whites alike fled to the industrial North, leaving the land to erode, the farms and villages to decay, and neighbor to mistrust neighbor.

So began the misery that was to last for one hundred years, despite the euphemism of the word "Reconstruction." And though giant steps have been taken since the historic Supreme Court decision of 1954, there is still a long and sad road the South must travel to catch up with the rest of the nation.

And catching up it is, much of the advancement being based on the switch from an agrarian to an industrial economy. But most important to the industrial growth of the South has been the formation of the giant Tennessee Valley Authority, whose dams and generators make available the huge blocks of essential low-cost electric power. From this power entire industries developed, especially aluminum, chemicals, and forest products. Deposits of coal, iron ore, and limestone were forged into a steel industry centering upon Birmingham. In addition, the dams slowed the erosion of the land and created hundreds of miles of new navigable waterways on the Tennessee River. As a result, cheap water transportation with an outlet to the Mississippi and Ohio rivers and the Gulf of Mexico became a reality for upper Alabama, Tennessee, and Kentucky. Rural electric cooperatives brought light to farmhouses and villages once entirely illuminated by candle and coal-oil and oil lamps. And textile plants, once mere runaways from New England, now stood on their own because they were near the raw materials for synthetic clothing fibers.

But what has helped the New South most of all is the change in southern attitudes on the part of both decision makers and ordinary people alike. A strong motivation for the sparkling modernization of Atlanta, Jacksonville, and other cities is the growing realization that this country can no longer afford to waste 10 or 15 percent of its work force through cruel, outmoded activities.

Down the Florida east coast, the changes are even more apparent. Jacksonville has built an architectural showcase of new buildings, including a fine new art museum. Its busy harbor will become even busier with the extension of the cross-Florida canal from the Intracoastal Waterway. The huge space complex at Cape Kennedy grows mightily, and Ph.D.'s probably now outnumber the farmers. Space launchings are commonplace, and the astronauts come and go practically unnoticed.

The beaches of Florida are still the great magnets for winter vacationers, and though the buildup of hotels, motels, guest houses, and high-rise apartments is enormous, there are still miles of virtually deserted beaches from the Carolinas to mid-Florida where one can still walk barefoot without danger of stepping on a rusted beer can or broken pop bottle.

Of course, in the Florida resort section, things are quite different. New hotels are thrown up annually, vying in outlandish concepts calculated to entice the tourist. And though the sun and sand are theoretically the lures for the millions who visit there each winter, it seems that as the hotels become more lavish in their décor, entertainment, and food, fewer people go out on the beaches, preferring to sun in deck chairs at poolside or at rumba lessons, while the ocean laps almost unnoticed at their feet. One gets the feeling that the visitors are waiting for the entire beach to become air-conditioned before venturing out on it.

But whatever direction, the South and the Southeast have changed radically, often unhappily and sometimes violently, in the decade past. Backwoods farms are surrendering to industrial parks, and computer factories are now being built where once the only sound was a bird whistling in the piney woods.

85

THE GREAT SMOKY MOUNTAINS of North Carolina provide a backdrop for Fontana Lake, backed by Fontana Dam on the Little Tennessee River. One of the uppermost of the TVA dams, it has not only supplied much needed electricity but has also halted the once-rampant soil erosion and provided a source of recreation.

86

THE COASTAL SWAMP near Savannah is laced with hundreds of creeks, inlets, and islands. The Intercoastal Waterway, serving as a protected channel for shallow-draft shipping, passes through this area. Here a fishing trawler moves along the waterway on its return from the Atlantic fishing grounds.

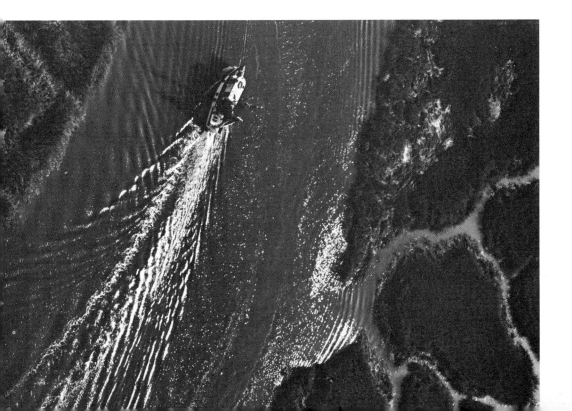

SAVANNAH, GEORGIA, oldest city in the state, is filled with gracious Regency and Georgian-styled buildings and attractive tree-lined squares facing the waterfront warehouses. On the bay side is historic Factors' Walk, a series of catwalks forming a promenade between the old cotton brokers' offices and Bay Street.

GEORGIA

ATLANTA'S SOARING NEW SKYLINE is dominated by the $175-million Peachtree Center, which has instilled a new pride in the citizens of this old southern capital. It consists of a new Merchandise Mart, several office buildings, and a beautiful new hotel, the Regency Hyatt House. The hotel has attracted national attention by its unusual design around a fully enclosed central court with spouting fountains and wall-scaling bubble elevators. The architect, John Portman, played a multiple role by designing the entire project, becoming its promoter and then hiring himself to supervise the construction to make sure all of his ideas were carried out.

88

PORTMAN'S ARCHITECTURAL VIRTUOSITY is graphically demonstrated by the dome treatment of the Regency (right), which contains a cocktail lounge and restaurant affording a spectacular view of the city. A second skylight over the main central court of the hotel brings light to the enclosed public areas. In the background, an aerial walkway connects the Atlanta Gas and the Merchandise Mart buildings. Future plans for Peachtree Center call for a group of high-rise apartments and a 70-story office tower plus the construction of underpasses to create a traffic-free pedestrian mall.

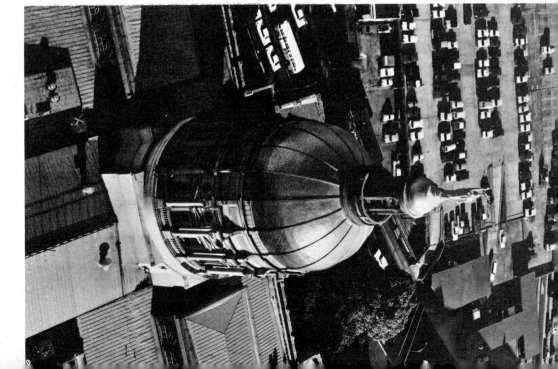

THE GILDED DOME of the state Capitol shines in the afternoon sun as counterpoint to the blue glass skylights of the Regency (below). This traditional executive chamber was constructed in 1889 and patterned after the national Capitol.

JACKSONVILLE, FLORIDA, is undergoing a wave of new construction, so far resulting in several fine buildings, like the prizewinning Gulf Life Building (right), an excellent riverfront recreational area, and a first-rate Art Museum. When the cross-Florida canal is completed, the direct connection with the Intracoastal Waterway is expected to bring a tremendous increase in Atlantic shipping.

ATLANTA STADIUM, newest addition to the sparkling modernization of the city. On a "game Sunday," it holds 60,000 smiling fans when any of its three major-league teams win and that many grouches when they lose.

FLORIDA EAST COAST

CASTILLO DE SAN MARCO (upper left) is better known as Fort St. Augustine, and is the oldest of its kind in the United States. It was near here that Ponce de León searched for the Fountain of Youth in 1513, a ritual still performed by thousands of college students each spring. As late as the Spanish-American War, the fort was used as a military prison, and is now a much-visited National Monument.

A DIFFERENT KIND OF FORTRESS is this swimming pool (left) at a hotel in Miami Beach that protects the coiffures of women guests from the surf of the adjoining ocean. And because their men are gallant, they obviously must keep their ladies company, and so the ocean is infrequently used. Thus the swimming pools of the hundreds of Miami Beach hotels become the daytime social centers, but the waters of the pools themselves are rarely disturbed by swimmers. One enterprising innkeeper, distressed by this state of affairs, put up a sign "Shark Free Pool!" to lure the swimmers in. Alas, all it attracted were the wolves who came in droves for the cha-cha lessons, canapés, and girl-watching.

THE JOHN F. KENNEDY SPACE CENTER is a down-to-earth complex consisting of the 15,000-acre Cape Kennedy test area and 88,000 acres on Merritt Island, all devoted to the space operations of NASA and the missile test programs of the Armed Forces. From these launch pads were blasted the Mercury and the Gemini capsules that carried our first astronauts into world orbit. The huge building at the upper left, seven miles away, is the Vehicle Assembly Building, part of Launch Complex 39 from which the Saturn rocket is expected to carry men to the moon. This 52-story-high building has the biggest room and the biggest window in the world, and is so vast in area space that it creates its own weather.

THE BEACHES OF NORTH FLORIDA are still relatively unpopulated and, for the most part, much as they were before Henry Flagler extended his railroad to Miami in 1896 and thus sparked the land boom still stirring the southern end of Florida. This beach is close to St. Augustine, and easily accessible for those who prefer the wild beauty and unspoiled stretches of open ocean and boiling surf.

MIAMI BEACH, by contrast, is so built up that one has the feeling that if any more hotels are erected the entire island will sink. Yet each year newer and more opulent structures are offered as monuments to the affluent who flock here annually for their vacations. This photograph was made from over 43rd Street looking north toward the Fontainebleau Hotel.

MIAMI

VIZCAYA, A VENETIAN PALACE built in Miami around 1912, is not a replica or a transplant from Italy, but an authentic Palazzo of the Renaissance period. It was built by John Deering, then president of the International Harvester Company, in a 30-acre mangrove swamp south of the city. Among its curiosities is a stone breakwater in the shape of a barge, a casino (foreground), a 17th-century Travertine marble fountain (upper right), many statues, all set on ten acres of formal gardens. Now operated by Dade County, it is open to the public for a fee.

THE CITY OF MIAMI is the major commercial center of southern Florida, and the largest city in the state. Though one tends to think of Miami Beach across Biscayne Bay as the tourism center, Miami itself is an important winter resort, and boasts an average of only six days each year without sunshine. Whether or not this is true, it does draw some five million tourists each year through its gates, and offers a wide variety of attractions in excellent beaches, cultural centers, a fine marine museum, water-sports facilities, and a broad range of first-class hotels.

THE MARINA AT DINNER KEY, just south of Miami's city center, can accommodate 166 small boats in its slips. With over 300 square miles of protected waters in Biscayne Bay and outlets to the Atlantic Ocean, sailing, powerboating, fishing, and water sports are a primary way of life for natives and tourists alike. The large building (right) that looks like an airplane hangar used to be home base for Pan American's old flying boats that first inaugurated service to Latin America.

THE PUBLIC BEACH AT KEY BISCAYNE, with its palm trees growing out of the sand, is a pleasant, relaxing place just a few minutes' drive over the Rickenbacker Causeway, which also crosses Virginia Key. Both keys are highly developed as public recreation areas to serve the combined needs of the tourist and permanent community. They hold a marine park with the usual performing porpoises, a water stadium, picnic grounds, and very attractive zoological gardens.

The Gulf Coast

THE GULF COAST, conjuring visions of Jean Lafitte, alligators, shrimp boats, jambalaya, New Orleans, live oak trees, and Longfellow's Evangeline country, stretches for nearly 2,000 miles from the tip of Florida to Mexico. For hundreds of years the Spanish, French, English, and the Indians occupied themselves as pirates, trappers, traders, and farmers. Later, their descendants became the oil explorers, roughnecks, spacemen, artists, writers, and bankers, all of whom helped change the Gulf Coast from steamy mangrove swamps, red clay farms, and cypress forests into an enormous complex of oil and petrochemical plants, busy ports, and bustling cities.

On the Florida west coast, the white beaches and warm waters of the Gulf of Mexico attract tourists and retirees, while at Tarpon Springs, Greek sponge fishermen have revived a once dying industry by equipping their colorful boats with modern diving gear even as they keep their old traditions.

As the coastline swings to the northwest, so does the economy swing in emphasis. Commerce through the ports of Mobile, Pascagoula, New Orleans, and Lake Charles accounts for a far greater dollar volume than the tourists following the Azalea Trail. Huge offshore oil rigs dot the Gulf, many of them self-contained small cities housing the men and equipment to bring up the oil, sulfur, and gas.

New Orleans is the hub of all this activity even as the new industries spread east and west of the Delta. If ever a city was ideal for writers, surely New Orleans must be second only to Paris, yet writers cannot seem to agree about it. Colonized in the 1700's by the French, transferred to Spanish rule and then back to French, and finally sold to the United States, the city shows marks of all these cultures and has added a few of its own. It is the gateway to Latin America, the terminus of the Mississippi River Basin, and sits at the crossroads of the Intracoastal Canal—that inglorious ditch that runs from Florida to Texas, and carries more tonnage than the Kiel or Panama canals. Some 15,000 miles of U.S. inland waterways revolve around New Orleans, making it the second largest American seaport.

But New Orleans is more than just a long line of piers and wharfs. With its universities and colleges, it is a great educational and medical training center. It's also a playground . . . but not for the sandbox set. Bourbon Street and paralleling Royal Street, in the heart of the French Quarter (or the Vieux Carré to those who have been there longer than twenty minutes), are just fourteen blocks long. But in these fourteen blocks are great restaurants, jazz joints, bars, some elegant and some less so, and fine hotels topped off by a lacy mantle of wrought-iron grill-

work, semitropical shrubbery, and historic buildings. At night Bourbon Street lights up, and the better restaurants, such as Galatoire's, Arnaud's, and Brennan's, quickly fill. A few of the old jazz bars, like the Paddock or the Famous Door, are still going strong, and Dixieland Hall, presenting fine traditional jazz, is the mecca for the visiting jazz buffs or the sideman who picks up a horn or the beat with a tap of his toe. Many consider an evening in New Orleans unfinished unless they stop by the French Market near the levee for the strong dark roast Louisiana coffee and hot fresh doughnuts.

By day Bourbon Street sleeps, and Royal Street comes to life with its antique shops, silversmiths, and art galleries. Sunday churchgoers leaving St. Louis Cathedral on Jackson Square usually head for one of the better restaurants for a traditional brunch apt to include Eggs Benedict, Lobster Bisque, Pompano en Papillote and a variety of wines.

Upriver to Baton Rouge, great petrochemical complexes take over sugarcane fields and spread westward through the rice country around Crowley. A new Interstate Highway points its concrete daggers at Baton Rouge but hesitates as if undecided about plunging through the Atchafalaya Swamp.

But even after the Interstate is completed (and there are many who hope it will never quite make it through the great swamp), knowledgeable travelers, local oilmen, and others will detour off it to Opelousas, a sleepy little town a few miles to the north to have lunch or dinner at Didie's. Rarely mentioned in the guidebooks but known to many, it serves the best oyster, chicken, or crab gumbo anywhere in the Cajun country. Traditionally for fifty years, fishermen, trappers, and oilmen have filled their fruit jars with this fiery mixture before taking their pirogues or launches out into the bayous.

Today the huge swamp retains much of its serenity. The cypress and live oak trees festooned with Spanish moss are a haven for the birds and teeming wildlife, undisturbed for the most part except for the slap of a paddle as a fisherman or trapper glides through the bayous, and for the occasional roar of a crew boat or marsh buggy bringing men and materials to one of the many oil wells deep in the interior.

Now, almost too late, are the conservationists being heard as the last of the bald cypresses are felled, and the chemical fumes kill the vegetation. For generations no one seemed to care that it takes at least four hundred years for a cypress to grow to maturity, and for a while no one seemed worried about their extinction. But now voices are being raised and battle lines are being formed, if not to stop progress, at least to make it livable.

99

FLORIDA WEST COAST

THE CITRUS GROVES of Florida march in orderly rows (right) over the flat sandy loam of this fast-growing state. Florida's climate, often considered its richest asset, is ideal for the citrus fruit industry, which accounts for $300 million of the state's annual agricultural market.

ST. PETERSBURG, FLORIDA, on the Gulf of Mexico, has been attracting a new breed of resident other than the traditional retiree or tourist looking for a quieter vacation spot. With an expanding industrial base around Tampa Bay, more families are seeking permanent havens on these man-made islands to enjoy the warm sunshine and Gulf waters.

ALABAMA

MOBILE, ALABAMA, on Mobile Bay, forty miles from the Gulf of Mexico, is Alabama's only seaport. Like most Gulf cities, it has seen a succession of French, Spanish, British, and American rules, and shows characteristics of each. Today, the busy port is host to carriers of all flags, with the huge Alabama State Docks supplying most of the wharfage space. In the foreground is the Alabama Drydock Company, and across the busy Mobile River is the city with its growing skyline.

DAUPHINE ISLAND ON MOBILE BAY has become more popular since the opening of a mainland causeway, but there are still many miles of unpopulated beaches, plus an Audubon Bird Sanctuary. Fort Gaines, and Fort Morgan across the entrance to the bay, both restored now, were used during the Civil War.

ISLE AUX OIES RIVER, or the Fowl River as it is known locally, is really a pleasant bayou flowing into Mobile Bay south of the port city, and is bordered by simple weekend cottages, comfortable homes, and elegant mansions. Nearly every family living here has at least one boat, and many a boathouse is built for two. Bellingrath Gardens, a beautiful subtropical park, is also located near here.

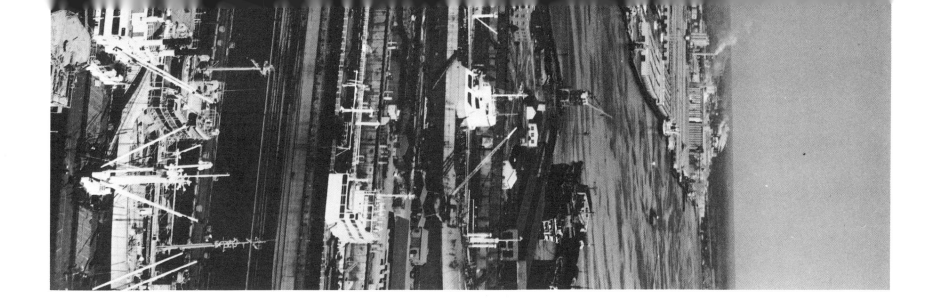

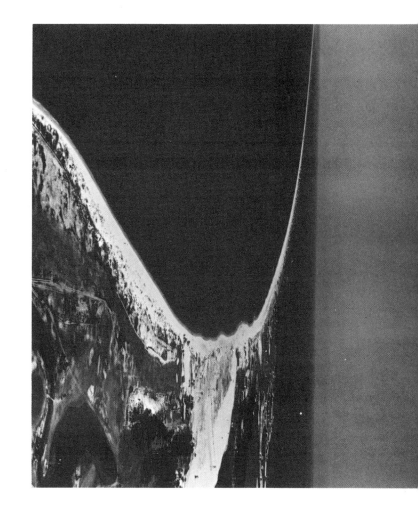

NEW ORLEANS

A TANKER PASSING NEW ORLEANS (upper left) as it moves along the winding Mississippi River to Baton Rouge, 120 miles upriver. The bridge in the foreground is part of a chain of expressways that links the Crescent City to the fast-growing national interstate system.

THE NEW ORLEANS CIVIC CENTER (left), west of the business district of the city, is a new complex of buildings encompassing City Hall, the Main Library, Court buildings, and the ultramodern Plaza Tower just across the way. In the background is part of the Medical Center, which contains Charity Hospital, the Tulane University Medical School, and a modern V.A. hospital. Farther back is part of the residential district northeast of Canal Street and Lake Pontchartrain.

THE NEW INTERNATIONAL TRADE MART (above), at the foot of Canal Street, rises next to the old ferry terminal, which still carries commuters to Algiers, across the river. In front of the building is the side-wheel steamer President, a sightseeing vessel. To the right are the Bienville Street wharf and other docks lining the river and part of the French Quarter. Canal Street, main thoroughfare of the city, angles to the upper right, and the main business district is on its left.

THE VIEUX CARRÉ, or the French Quarter, is New Orleans' most famous area, and often the first stop for visitors. It is dominated by Jackson Square and the St. Louis Cathedral. The Cabildo (left of Cathedral) was once the residence of the Spanish governors, and the Presbytère (to the right) is now a museum. Flanking the square are the Pontalba Apartments, said to be the oldest apartment houses in America. The two large buildings in the upper left are a county office building and The Royal Orleans Hotel. The character of the Quarter is carefully preserved by the Vieux Carré Commission, which sees to it that the old buildings are kept in good repair and that new ones are in keeping with the traditional architecture. The French Market with its popular coffee stalls is in the lower left.

THE CEMETERIES OF NEW ORLEANS are aboveground crypts because the water table is so high that it would be impossible to place the vaults below ground level. As a result this burial ground looks more like the pattern of a large city photographed from high altitude. There are many of these graveyards inside the city limits, several within the French Quarter area; but this one is out on Canal Street near the big City Park.

THIS CHARMING STEAMBOAT GOTHIC house is one of two identical structures just behind the levee on Egania Street. The ornamentation garlanding the building and the simulated pilothouse at the top reflect the love for the river that the owner, Captain Milton Doullut, a shipbuilder and river pilot, must have felt when he, his son Paul, and a Negro helper put it up in 1905. Paul built a duplicate one for himself a block away in 1914, and both houses are still occupied by the descendants of the original builders.

OAK ALLEY PLANTATION house at Vacherie on the west bank of the Mississippi above New Orleans is typical of the Greek Revival style of great plantation houses that were built along the river in the 1830's. This one is noted for its beautiful grove of live-oak trees reaching from the Mississippi to the house and beyond.

LOUISIANA

SUGARCANE FIELDS on both banks of the river above New Orleans are kept in neat rows so that they may be harvested by machine instead of by the hand labor of by-gone days. This field is at Reserve, near Lake Pontchartrain.

ANOTHER GREEK REVIVAL style building is Longue Vue, the beautiful home of Mrs. Edgar B. Stern, noted philanthropist and civic leader in New Orleans. Though built considerably later than Oak Alley above, and set in handsome formal gardens instead of the stands of live oaks, it conveys the same feeling of spaciousness and comfort of the southern classic plantation houses.

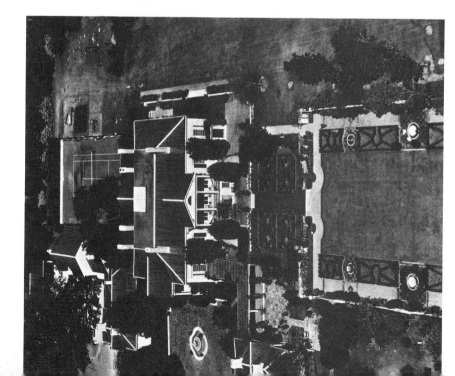

110

THE SHELL OIL COMPANY REFINERY at Norco on the Mississippi above New Orleans and the other two plants on stream across the river are typical of vast changes that have come over this once predominantly agricultural area. These plants produce a vast array of petroleum and chemical products from the huge underground reserves of gas, oil, salt, and sulfur, and the resulting industrialization has reshaped the Gulf states' economy and revitalized the entire region.

THE SAN FRANCISCO PLANTATION house at Reserve, in the heart of Louisiana's sugarcane country, was built in 1849 in the baroque Steamboat Gothic tradition. It has been restored, filled with 18th-century antiques, and opened to the public. The house was constructed behind a levee for protection against the often rampaging river, while the willows in the foreground reach down to the water's edge, and the sugarcane fields in the background are still actively cultivated.

112

THE LAKE PONTCHARTRAIN CAUSEWAY is the longest highway bridge over water in the world. Stretching for thirty-one miles from New Orleans to the cypress swamps of St. Tammany Parish across the lake, a motorist is actually out of sight of land for almost eight miles. Once north of the lake, the causeway heads into Mississippi to connect with other east and west highways.

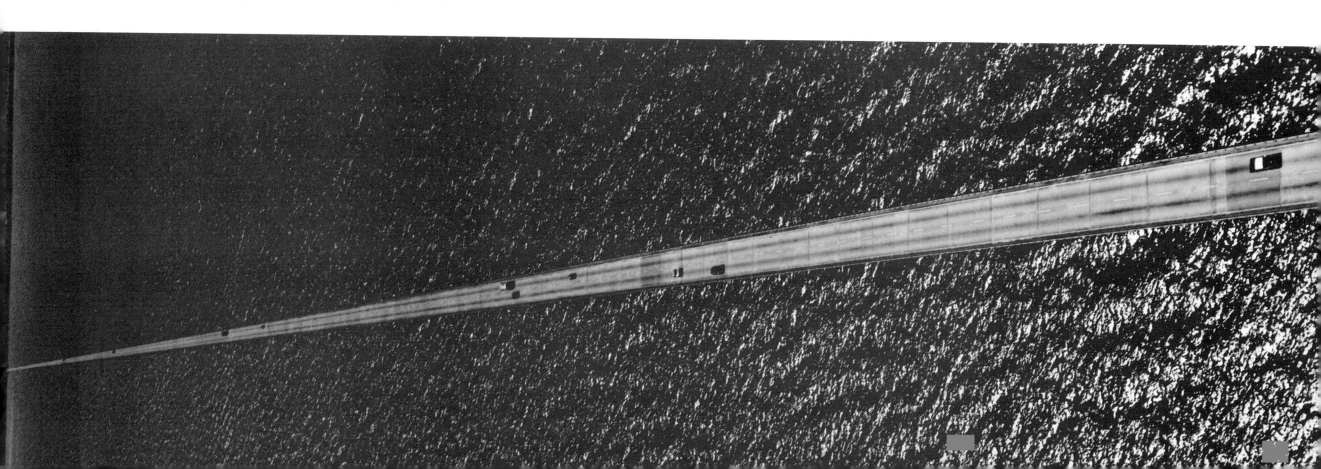

MISSISSIPPI

A WATERHOLE ON A FARM near Liberty, Mississippi. Unlike the highway bridge at the left which archaeologists a thousand years from now can accurately date because cars or architecture are artifacts of time and place, this scene is ageless. Will a man sit in a saddle or will his horse drink any differently in fifty years' time, or will a cow amble across a lane in a manner at all different from the one seen at the top of this photograph taken by me approximately twenty years ago?

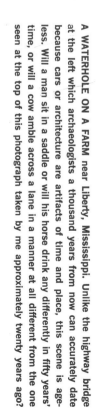

115

A FARM NEAR NATCHEZ. Like the picture on the preceding page, this photograph was made many years ago, during the course of a flight in a pipeline patrol plane. But in October, 1967, I flew over the same area, and there has been little change in the landscape or in the looks of the small farms still isolated from the tempo of traffic and urban life.

OFF THE COAST OF LOUISIANA, these double offshore rigs probe for oil in the bottom of the Gulf of Mexico. They are sophisticated structures, costing several millions of dollars each, and can drill a number of wells from the same location. Each has its own helicopter landing pad, its own crew quarters, kitchen, dining and limited recreation facilities. These offshore rigs are movable to other drilling sites in the ever-widening search for new sources of petroleum. The drilling pipe, tools, and supplies are brought in by the tenders, and the oil is taken off either in barges or pipelines, depending upon the depth of water and distance offshore. When tropical hurricanes sweep through the Gulf, as they often do in the fall, the men are quickly evacuated to the mainland by helicopters.

The Southwest

THE IMAGES OF THE SOUTHWEST are probably more actively perpetuated than those of any other single region in North America. Think of the Southwest, and you get pictures of cowboys and Indians, gold prospectors, oil wildcatters, and wheeling-dealing Texans—none of them very much in the background. And with good reason, for the Southwest is a vast and colorful area, containing, save for two, the last of the states admitted to the Union. And even in the 1960's, memories of the wild land rushes, oil strikes, and cattle roundups are still fairly fresh in the minds of many living Americans. Add to that the millions of feet of horse operas depicting the Good Guys and Bad Guys that have been standard motion-picture fare since motion pictures were invented (and rerun endlessly on TV late shows), and you have a virtually endless supply of reminders about how it's supposed to be in the Southwest.

But in spite of the usual images of vast plains, dry gulches, and thundering herds of cattle, there are other faces of the Southwest. The lush and verdant bayous of East Texas are a far cry from the spectacular coppery sandstone of the Grand Canyon with the surprising green stripe of Colorado River winding along the bottom. The golden wheat fields of the Oklahoma and Texas Panhandle, with their nearby grain elevators starkly silhouetted at the railroad sidings, are in marked contrast to the southern Rockies that extend into New Mexico. And all these wide-open spaces serve as balances to the huge refineries and the industrial centers, making everything from Airplanes to Zinc.

But most surprising to those who think of the Southwest in traditional terms is the sight of modern cities rising from the flat plains, showing a freshness and vitality that seem to set them apart from other urban centers of equal size and population. Perhaps this results from an effort to diminish the frontier image or to get away from the overworked "bigger than everything" concept, but urban Southwesterners are more frequently apt to point with pride to new theatres, art galleries, universities, and medical centers than to the expected cattle spreads, oil fields, and petrochemical complexes.

Agriculture, too, has changed in this region, and the change has had a major impact on the area's economy. Citrus fruits, always big business in Florida and California, have become major crops in Texas and Arizona. Cotton, once King in the Southeast, has now expanded into large tracts of irrigated land in the Southwest, seeded, weeded, and harvested by machines.

But most important to the economic growth of the Southwest has been the production of oil and gas, closely followed by copper, potash, uranium, and other minerals upon which the entire world depends.

Culturally, there would seem to be no lack of recognition of the Spanish and Indian heritage, if you choose to judge by the number of motels called El Rancho, La Hacienda, Navaho or Apache. But, until recently, the identification almost stopped there, for both Indians and Spanish-Americans are often discriminated against and left to wither or fend for themselves on primitive reservations or in ghetto-like shantytowns.

But as mores are changing in the South and Northeast regarding Negroes, so too are they beginning to change in the Southwest. A good example was the handling of the oil and gas discovery on the Navaho Reservation at Four Corners (the intersection of the state lines of Colorado, Utah, Arizona, and New Mexico). Instead of the usual senseless distribution of minimal oil royalties on a head basis, the Navaho Tribal Council acted to retain a higher percentage of oil royalties for the tribe as a whole, and pool these monies in sizable blocks to be reinvested, over and above the pitiful grants doled out by the Bureau of Indian Affairs, for either communal projects, such as irrigation, electrification, or higher education, or economic ventures such as sawmills or power plants.

By establishing a broader base of security for the Indian who wants to leave the reservation for a place in contemporary America, there is a new promise shaping the Indian community, and the outlook is brighter than ever before. This was graphically illustrated by a comparison of two scenes I observed—the first a few years back in front of a Navaho trading post, where two small blue-jeaned Indian boys, who had obviously seen too many TV Westerns, were attempting to play cowboys and Indians. But they had some trouble in that neither wanted to play the Indian. The other incident happened last year when, while driving through a large Indian-owned grazing area, I was suddenly engulfed by a huge flock of baaing sheep. But the Indian herders were not mounted on horses, as I fully expected, but riding instead in separate new Jeeps, complete with two-way radio communication between the cars and the ranch, and the language they used was pure Navaho.

If these are signs of changing times, there are similar ones in the non-Indian world. As more factories spread through the Southwest border states, and as the copper, gold, silver, and zinc refineries are expanded, more jobs are being opened to the Spanish-Americans who previously had to make do with low-paying and backbreaking stoop-labor agricultural jobs. And as computers and other electronic instrument plants are sprouting in many places throughout the Southwest, the precision of the needlework skills handed down through generations of Spanish-American women is a sizable asset in the assembly of delicate electronic parts.

Moreover, many people who in recent years flocked to the Southwest for reasons of health, climate, or pleasure stayed on to settle and be productive in this newest part of the United States.

OKLAHOMA

THE ROUNDHOUSE AT EL RENO, OKLAHOMA, is now only a memory of the steam railroading days when the buffs talked knowledgably of 4-6-2's, double headers, or Mallet-class engines. Then, no matter how long one worked around a roundhouse, there would always be a pause as the big turntable in the center swung its load around and pointed a big one into a stall. Today, America's railroads have converted to diesels that are serviced in prosaic straight-line sheds, pausing only long enough to pick up fuel, sand, and water before continuing on their runs. If the diesels are more efficient, they are less colorful, and the passing of the steam engine is mourned by all who heard its big whistle moaning for a crossing in the middle of the night or saw the cloud of steam etched across a clear blue winter sky.

FORTY-ACRE SPACING OF OIL WELLS is a conservation method adopted by oil-producing Oklahoma to control overproduction in the oil fields. In some cases, eighty acres of spacing is required to conserve even further the pools of oil and gas. In this wheatfield near Tulsa, the big rig will drill down almost three miles before being disassembled and relocated. If a producing well is completed, a "Christmas Tree" (a series of valves and controls connecting the well with a pipeline) will be erected; or, if the well is a "dry hole" or a "duster," it will be plugged, capped, and land restored, the debris removed, and the "roughnecks" will move the rig to a new site.

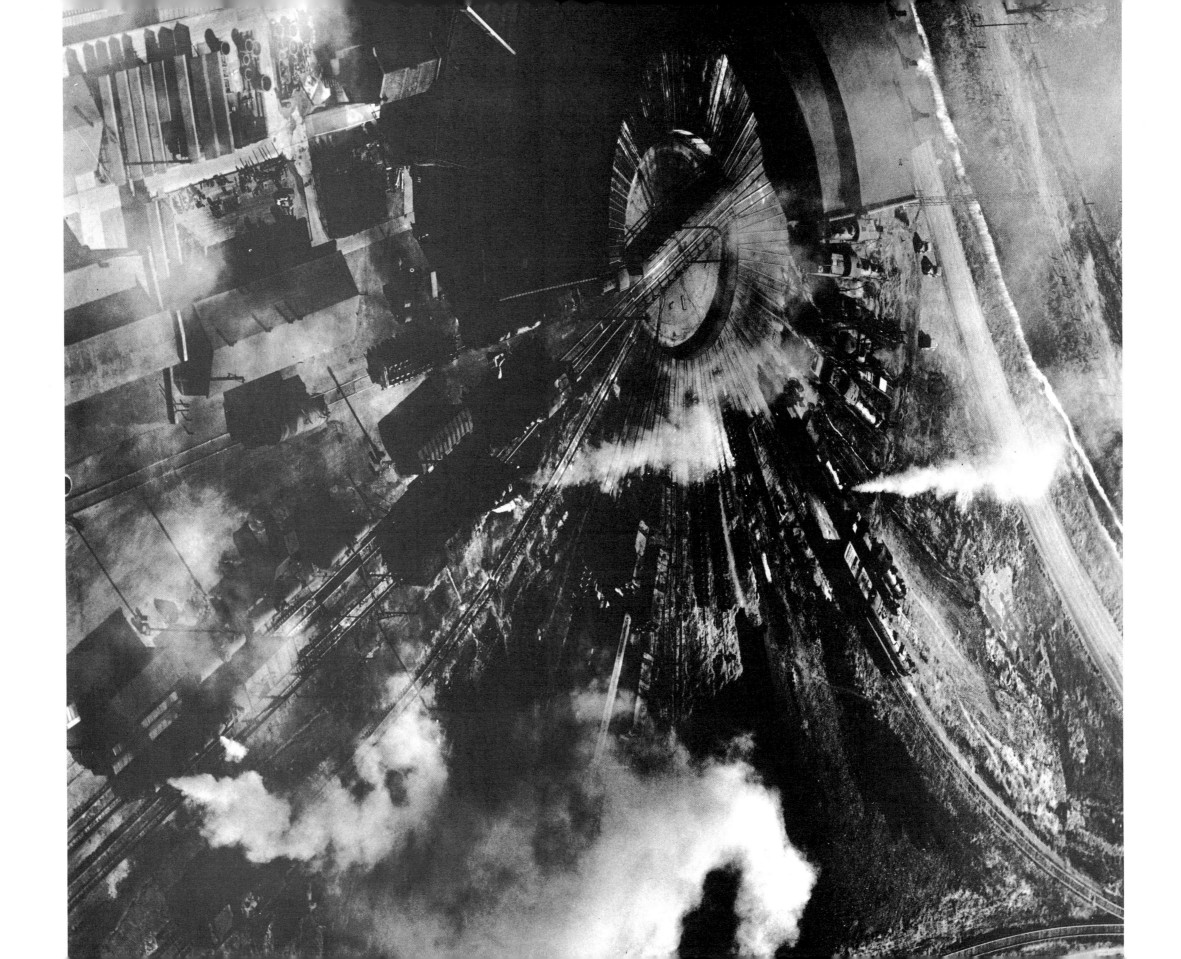

HOUSTON

JONES HALL FOR THE PERFORMING ARTS in downtown Houston provides the proper atmosphere for its first-rate symphony orchestra and visiting musical groups. Nearby Music Hall and the new Hall of Exhibits all contribute to the city's growing cultural influence in the world of the arts.

HOUSTON'S ASTRODOME is an enormous fully enclosed arena (top) that can seat 66,000 spectators in its air-conditioned and post-free stands. But even the best of plans can go awry, as the engineers discovered when the 5,000 plastic skylights in the roof threw so much glare back at the ballplayers that they kept losing the ball. Ultimately, the panes had to be blacked over and then the grass didn't grow.

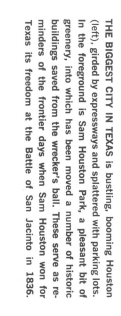

THE BIGGEST CITY IN TEXAS is bustling, booming Houston (left), girded by expressways and splattered with parking lots. In the foreground is Sam Houston Park, a pleasant bit of greenery, into which has been moved a number of historic buildings saved from the wrecker's ball. These serve as reminders of the frontier days when Sam Houston won for Texas its freedom at the Battle of San Jacinto in 1836.

123

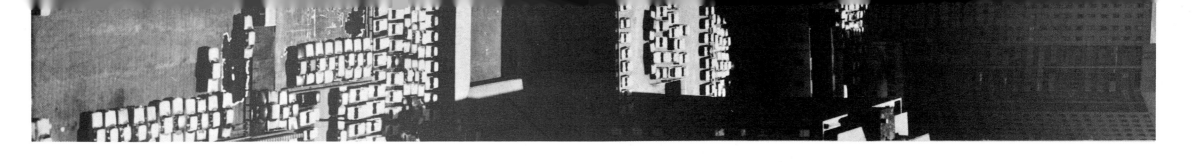

DALLAS

WALL-TO-WALL PARKING is the hallmark of many a city without mass transit facilities. Dallas (left), like many other fast-growing cities, is almost wholly dependent on the automobile for moving its people to and from work. The saving factor is an intricate system of expressways that transport the vast herds of automobiles rapidly, with a fair amount of room still available for parking. But as the number of cars increases, it is evident that some important new method of moving people is going to have to be developed. If not, the populace will have to face up to the thought of walking, an idea that some sociologists insist has already been discarded by many motor-borne Americans around the nation.

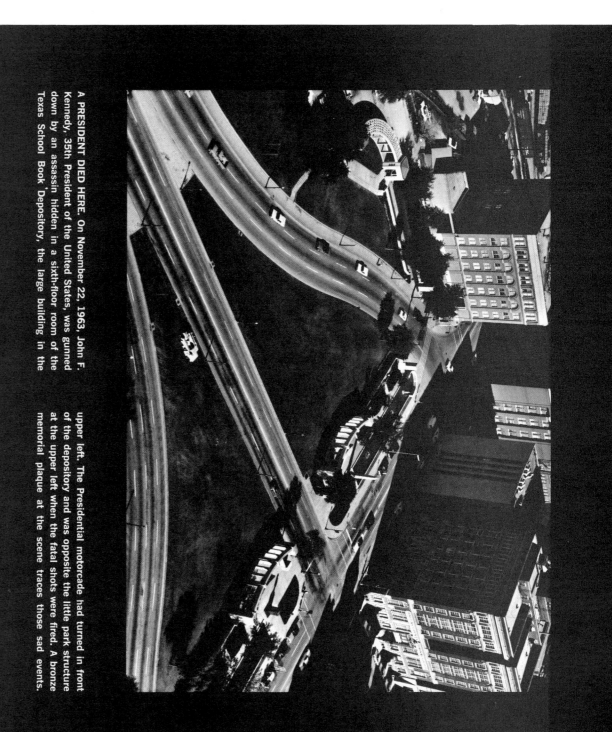

A PRESIDENT DIED HERE. On November 22, 1963, John F. Kennedy, 35th President of the United States, was gunned down by an assassin hidden in a sixth-floor room of the Texas School Book Depository, the large building in the upper left. The Presidential motorcade had turned in front of the depository and was opposite the little park structure at the upper left when the fatal shots were fired. A bronze memorial plaque at the scene traces those sad events.

THE BOLD NEW SKYLINE of Dallas soars over the Texas prairie, a far cry from the cattle town that was chartered as a city less than a hundred years ago. Big "D," as the natives call it, is now a major manufacturing center for aircraft, automobiles, oil-field equipment, and farm machinery. Nor has it neglected its cultural side. The Margo Jones Theatre, the nation's oldest theatre-in-the-round, a fine symphony orchestra, a civic opera company, several good museums, and major universities all contribute to making this one of the most vital cities in the Southwest.

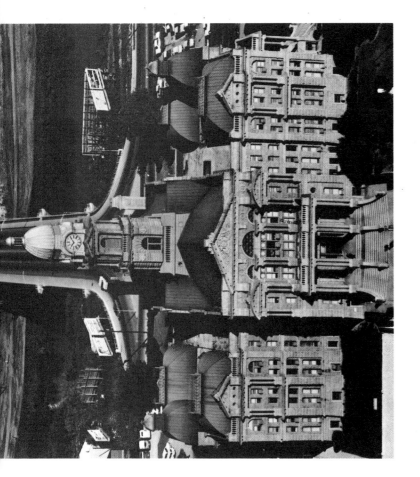

FORT WORTH

FORT WORTH'S COURTHOUSE continues to retain its baroque splendor as it stands with its back to the Trinity River and seems to hold off encroaching skyscrapers, expressways, and other signs of "progress."

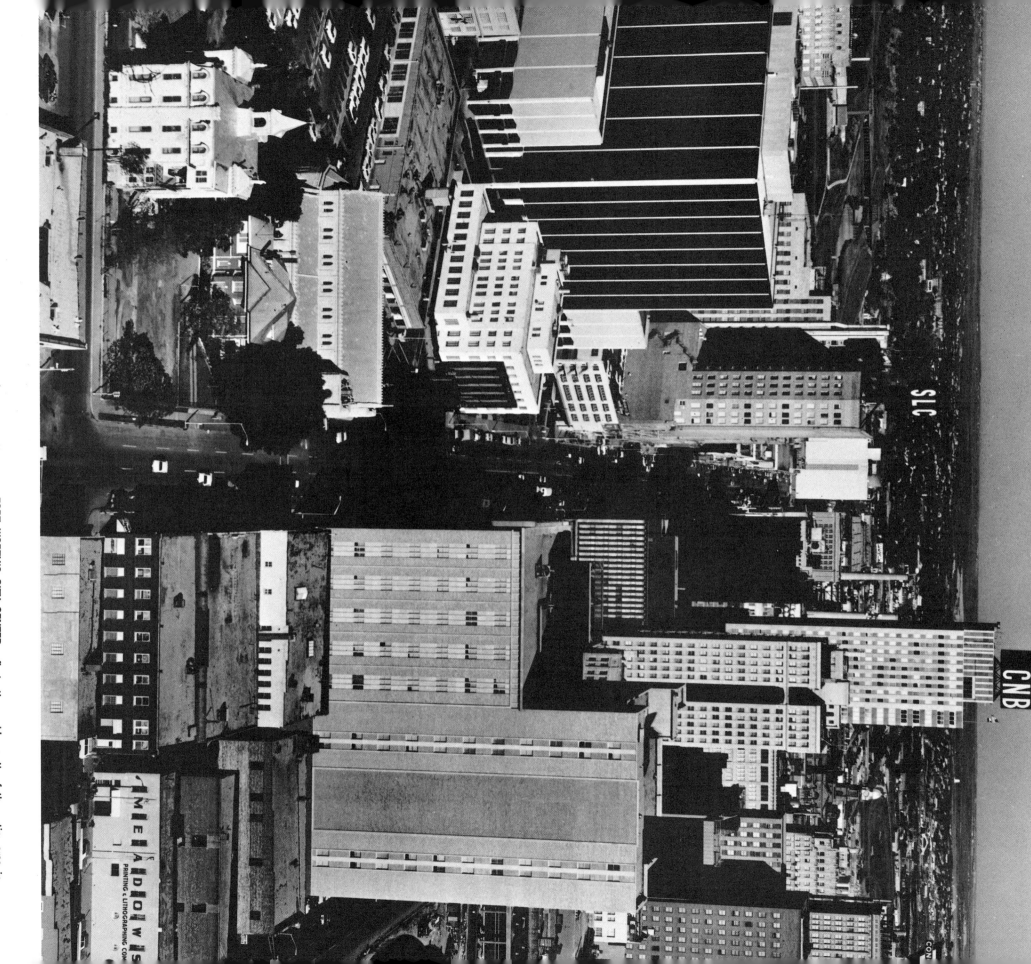

THE STOCKYARDS AT FORT WORTH, a throwback to its early days as a cattle center, continue to be a prime source of commerce for this city thirty miles to the west of Dallas. But its residents, in trying to live down the title of "cowtown," have hastened to build a clutch of new skyscrapers, a huge convention center, and a booming aircraft-manufacturing industry, including the big Bell Helicopter Company plant and several producers of military aircraft and related components.

FORT WORTH'S CITY CENTER reflects the rapid growth of the entire area in the hundred years since it was first settled as an army post against Indian attack. Surrounding the city are many lakes, some of them man-made, which provide a vast recreation area for the thousands of workers in the big aircraft plants, refineries, railroad repair shops, meatpacking plants, and grain elevators who have helped Fort Worth grow into a metropolitan complex of 600,000 people.

129

THE TEXAS PANHANDLE, near Amarillo, is a vast wheat and cattle country with weather so severe that ranchers often say there is nothing but a barbed-wire fence between the panhandle and Alaska to ward off the frigid wintry blasts when a "blue norther" comes down. Here one really feels the vastness of West Texas; a ranch or wheat spread is thought of in thousands of acres; the tallest building is apt to be a grain elevator; and to visit a neighbor may require a half-hour's drive.

ARIZONA

PHOENIX, ARIZONA, IN THE SALT RIVER Valley, has grown into a major metropolis with modern high-rise buildings stretching for miles along **Central Avenue,** the principal north-south artery. The warm winter climate, fed by the hot dry desert air, has attracted many people who initially came for vacation or health reasons, and stayed on to become productive residents turning out a variety of manufactured items from aluminum extrusions to computers and aircraft parts.

132

A HORSE RANCH NEAR SCOTTSDALE is a pastoral setting in the desert, only a short drive from downtown Phoenix. While the horses raised here are no longer used to haul stagecoaches or remount the pony-express riders, many of the West's oldest traditions are maintained in modern Arizona. Broad-brimmed Stetsons are still necessary to shield a rancher's neck from the hot sun, and many prospectors for uranium, copper, silver, or lead have outfitted here.

133

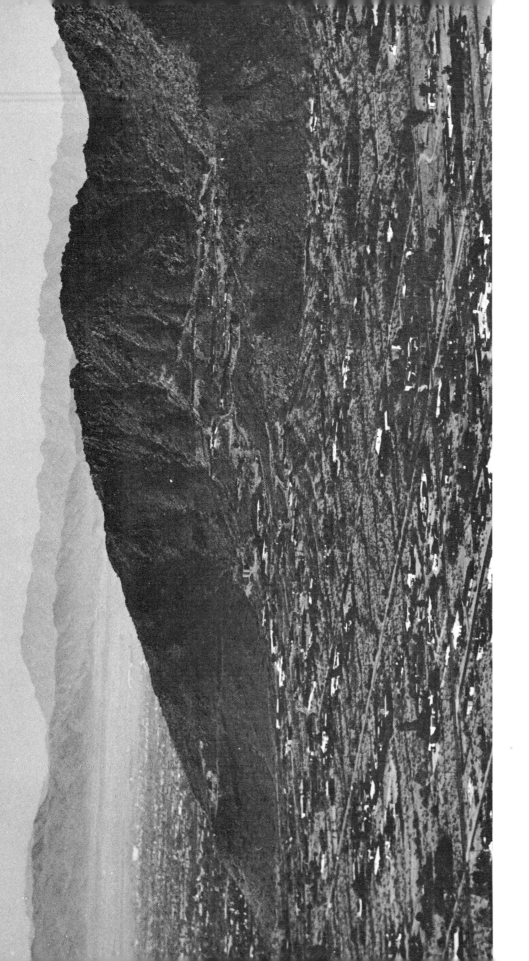

CAMELBACK MOUNTAIN IN SCOTTSDALE is a famous landmark in this residential community near Phoenix. Much of the resort industry is in nearby Paradise Valley, and the region is laced with luxurious hotels and inns. While few horses are still used, local law requires that automobiles give them right of way. The downtown section of the city is patterned after the Old West, with false-front stores and frontier "saloons" barely concealing some elegant boutiques.

SUN CITY, A RETIREMENT COMMUNITY not far from Phoenix, has added a new dimension to this expanding area. Vast tracts have been developed of air-conditioned houses, golf courses, swimming pools, and craft shops designed to attract the retiree to the superb Arizona climate. One such resident celebrated his occupancy by permanently embedding his lawn mower in concrete, and creating a "lawn" of gravel, dyed grass-green, that never needs cutting or watering.

ARIZONA STATE UNIVERSITY, set on a handsome campus near Phoenix, is a fully accredited university with colleges of liberal and applied arts and schools of nursing, engineering, and architecture. The School of Agriculture has an excellent example to follow right in its own front yard, because the beautiful round structure in the foreground with the soaring approach ramps and the scalloped trim was designed by the eminent architectural master Frank Lloyd Wright.

TALIESIN WEST, IN THE PARADISE VALLEY northwest of Phoenix, is another Frank Lloyd Wright structure. But instead of being designed for a client, this building was created for the Taliesin Fellowship, a school for architectural apprentices who came to live and work with Wright himself. The building is constructed of masonry and redwood timber, and, while it shows the individualistic stamp of Wright, the influence of terrain and regional history is also evident.

NEW MEXICO

THE MISSION CHURCH of St. Francis Assisi at the Ranchos de Taos, four miles south of the town of Taos, is one of the oldest Spanish Mission churches in continuous use in the Southwest. Built between 1710 and 1755, it is made of adobe, with walls six feet thick. Taos itself has become a major art center, with some 100 artists in permanent residence, and scores more in the summertime. Nearby, Kit Carson National Forest is an ideal camping and outdoor recreation spot, with a number of major ski centers at neighboring Angel Fire and Red River.

THE RIO GRANDE GORGE near Taos is spanned by a new bridge that is locally called the "bridge to nowhere," but hopefully will connect Taos with a major east-west route. Here the Rio Grande River, whose headwaters are in Colorado and which becomes the border between Texas and Mexico farther south, cuts a deep and spectacular gorge in the high plains.

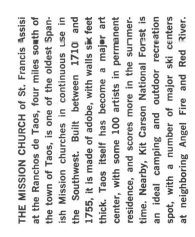

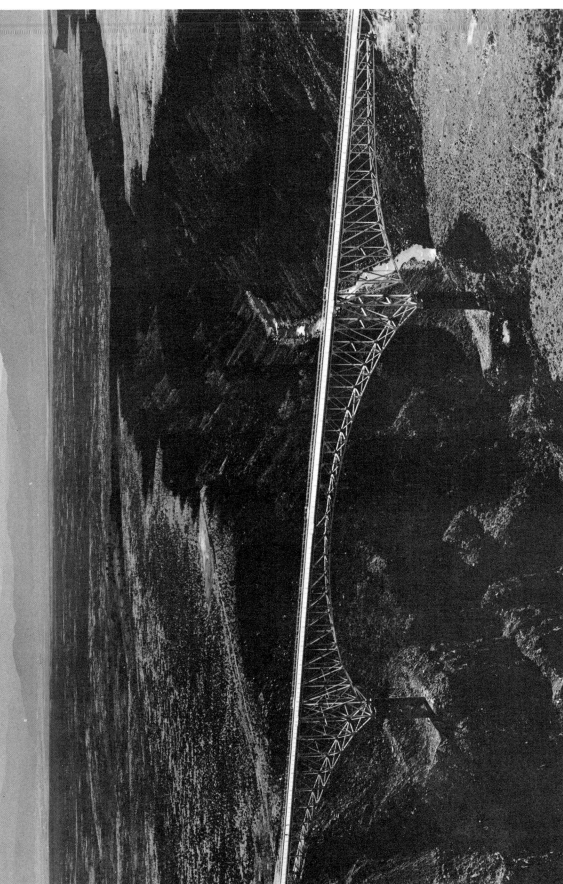

The Mountain West

LONG BEFORE A MOTORIST nears Denver from the east, he sees the towering peaks of the Rockies, and as the speeds toward them over the flat country of Kansas and the rolling land of eastern Colorado, he must certainly give pause and reflect on the rugged pioneers who crossed this then trackless waste in their Conestoga Wagons, on horses, or even on foot. These mountains must have appeared to be a near-impenetrable barrier. Perhaps it was for this reason that so many would-be miners and prospectors for the legendary silver and gold gave up and settled instead in Denver and nearby communities to become the tradesmen and suppliers for the more hardy strains who pushed on through the mountain passes.

Similarly, other settlers moved across Wyoming, over the Rattlesnake Range, skirted the Big Horns, and crossed the Wind River Range at a more modest elevation of 7,500 feet, nestled between the 10,000-foot summits on either side. Here the Oregon Trail went through to the gold fields of the West, the Pony Express was established, and the Union Pacific pushed its steel westward to cross the Continental Divide. Once over the Divide (that point where the rivers on the east side flow easterly and those on the west flow to the west), they came to the high plateau that reaches into Utah and the Snake and Green River valleys, whose lush grasslands, watered by the mountain snows, became the settling places for the sheep and cattle men. Through the Wasatch Mountains in northern Utah also came Brigham Young, Apostle of the Mormon Church who on July 23, 1847, led his followers into the beautiful valley east of the Great Salt Lake and uttered his historic "This is the place!" There they established their community after a wearing trek of 1,500 miles from Illinois and Missouri.

Because the ground was hard, so hard that it shattered their wooden plows, the farmers built small dams to divert the snow runoff into the fields to soften the soil so they could till it. From these simple beginnings came the vast irrigation systems that trapped the mountain waters and turned the deserts into productive farms and grazing areas.

But it was the miners who really opened the Mountain West. Many had rushed to the gold fields of California, only to find the better claims already staked or the lodes unproductive. Therefore many turned eastward to the mountains in the belief that they held silver and gold. By dint of backbreaking work with primitive tools, they uncovered the Comstock Lode in Virginia City, Nevada, that fabulous hole in the ground that was ultimately to yield more than $400 million worth of silver. Other miners found more treasure in the vast deposits of copper, lead, and zinc all through the mountains from Montana and Idaho in

the north to Arizona and New Mexico in the south. In fact it would seem that the entire Mountain West was busy digging the shafts, drifts, and stopes that made mining the largest part of the economy. Butte sits on a mountain of copper ore, and Kennecott's huge Bingham Canyon Mine near Salt Lake City is the world's largest open-pit copper mine. Molybdenum, potash, and uranium are also extracted, and nearly all of the gold produced in the United States is refined as a by-product from these ores. The underground mines are deep, some of them going down nearly a mile. The miners are a tough, independent breed who often work full shifts in water up to their waists or in choking dust or in steamy heat that frequently rises to well over a hundred degrees or more at the mine face. Underground the ore is richer, but impossible to tap except by drilling, blasting, and mucking. New machinery has helped enormously, but it's a backbreaking, dirty job fraught with danger of cave-ins, explosions, and respiratory disease.

The open pits are quite different. Here the problem is to move as much ore as possible, because to extract enough copper for a single 16-ounce skillet, over 500 pounds of ore and waste must be moved, processed, and refined. In fact, without the huge earthmoving equipment, trucks that carry 100 tons at a time on tires 8 feet in diameter, or electric power shovels that scoop out 12 cubic yards at one bite, mining these ores would be unprofitable. The whole operation is of such Paul Bunyanesque stature that entire railroad trains full of ore look like toys from Bingham Canyon across the 2-mile width.

While mining is still the mainstay of the Mountain West's economy, it's beginning to feel the hot breath of change, by the big push in tourism. The year-round snows in the mountains of Utah and Colorado have had the same lure as in New England. Cultural activities make the Mountain States a haven for the summer vacationer who attends a seminar or concert at Aspen, hears the Mormon Tabernacle Choir in the acoustically perfect hall in Salt Lake City, or feasts his eyes on the new architecture at the Air Force Academy at Colorado Springs.

But camping and fishing still come first, and any attempt to make a left turn on a mountain highway on a Sunday may take hours because of the never-ending stream of campers.

For the less hardy there are the epidermal attractions of Las Vegas or Reno or the never-closing gambling casinos, though it does take stamina to pull those slot-machine handles all night. But whatever his pleasure, should he ever feel a little smug about his trappings, he need only look at the ever-present sheepherders' wagons with their little stoves to remember that for many this is still the way of life in much of the Mountain West.

COLORADO

THE BATTLE FOR PRIVACY is drawn as urban sprawl sweeps across the flat land just west of Denver and halts at the perimeters of the lovely Helen Bonfils estate, just west of Denver and halts at the perimeters of the lovely Helen Bonfils estate, founding family of the Denver "Post." With its back to the encroaching supermarkets and shopping centers, it seems to say "Stand back!" and appears to be literally in a last-ditch fight to retain its gracious splendor before being pushed into the lake.

DOWNTOWN DENVER (left) sprouts a whole new facade of buildings in the $100-million Mile High Center, but keeps an island of serenity in the Civic Center with its lovely Memorial Colonnade and charming Greek Theatre. Denverites love their outdoors, as demonstrated by the city chain of public parks, which covers 25,000 acres of mountain grounds in 49 separate locations, as far away as 50 miles west and 20 miles south.

DENVER'S IMPRESSIVE SKYLINE (right) is matched by the Rocky Mountains to the west, rising from 5,000 to more than 14,000 feet within 50 miles from the city. The Colorado state Capitol on the left is topped by a dome covered with 24-carat gold leaf, a gift of its citizens honoring the mining industry.

141

AN ULTRAMODERN HOUSE, perched on the summit of 8,000-foot Genesee Mountain 25 miles west of Denver, commands a spectacular panoramic view of the majestic terrain. Built for his own use by architect Charles Deaton, who is also an inventor and industrial designer, this structure has attracted attention far beyond its native Denver, and has been likened to a bird poised for flight, an opening clam shell, or a flying saucer. It is none of these things, but only a demonstration of Deaton's desire to break away from the conventional form of house design and to express his considerable creative talents in functional architecture.

THE SPECTACULAR VALLEYS of the Rocky Mountain foothills west of Denver are the lures for thousands of outdoor-loving people who journey the year around to camp, fish, ski, and hunt. But recreation has not always been the way of life in the mountains, for they are honeycombed with mine tunnels, the now cold trails of men who dug deep into the hills in search of gold, silver, and lead. And when pay dirt was struck, as it often was, much of the reward would be spent on elegant houses and furnishings, sometimes transported piece by piece from Europe, or in the building of secluded turreted castles like the one below, or in the erection of opera houses, theatres, elaborate bars, saloons, and hunting lodges.

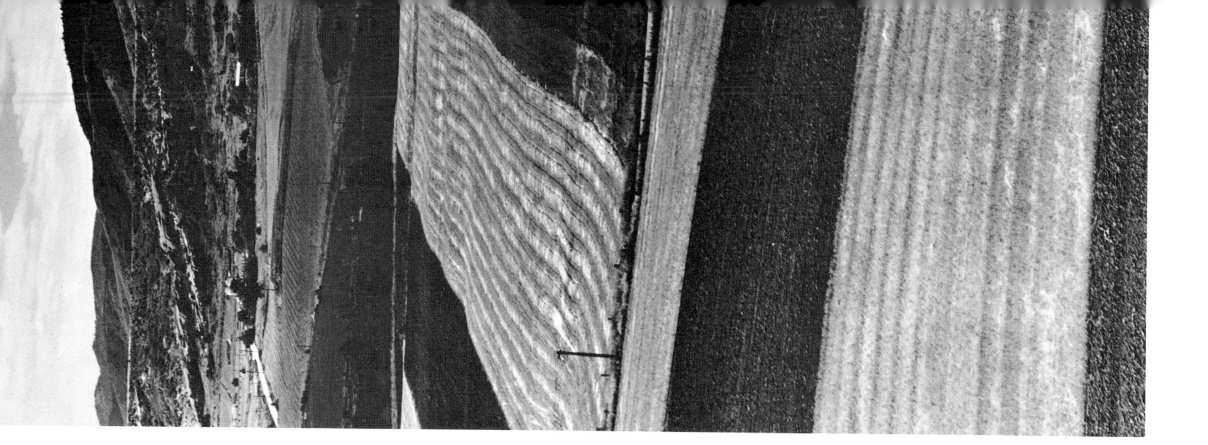

WHEAT FARMING IN THE FOOTHILLS of the Rockies west of Denver is performed on a smaller scale than on the big 640-acre sections of the Dakotas and the high plains east of Denver. But the ground here is particularly fertile because the snow runoff provides ample moisture, and makes unnecessary the complex irrigation systems used in the more arid parts of the state. This method of dry farming leaves broad strips of land fallow on alternate years to conserve the minerals in the soil and to control erosion. The widths of the strips vary with the terrain, and the directions are often changed to follow the contour of the ground.

A COMBINE BEGINS HARVESTING a wheat field on the east slope of the Rockies. This machine is a fairly modest-sized one; some have front cutter bars twenty feet wide. The name "combine" comes from the multiple operations it can perform, such as cutting, threshing, and cleaning a wide variety of grains and legumes. It can blow the wheat through a chute into a truck following alongside or it can bale hay or scatter it by a spreader, thus making itself indispensable for modern farming. On the big spreads, the combines will often harvest and glean the fields in gangs of three or four; the equipment is extremely sophisticated, many units having air conditioning, two-way radio communication, and big batteries of night lights for round-the-clock work during the critical harvest period.

THE STATE CAPITOL of Utah, at Salt Lake City, stands on a hillside overlooking this metropolis of broad avenues and large rambling houses. Lying in a valley west of the Wasatch Mountains and east of the Great Salt Lake, it is an important mining and distribution center because of its mutual proximity to the copper-mining, refining, and processing centers at Bingham Canyon and Magna, and the steel and coal areas around Provo, to the south. And because it is close to the excellent ski slopes at Alta and Park City, in addition to the spectacular gorges of the Colorado and Green rivers, Salt Lake City has also turned into a major tourist and recreational attraction.

THE MORMON TABERNACLE in Temple Square in Salt Lake City is the headquarters of the Church of Jesus Christ of Latter-Day Saints (or the Mormons). This important religious group was led to Utah in 1847 by Apostle Brigham Young, after a wearying trek from earlier settlements in the Midwest in search of religious freedom. An industrious people, they soon brought the valley under intense cultivation and, in the spirit of communal living (which included polygamy, later abandoned), established Salt Lake City. The Temple grounds and acoustically perfect auditorium housing the famous Tabernacle Choir are open to the public, though the Temple is not.

● THE GREAT OPEN-PIT COPPER MINE at Bingham Canyon, thirty miles from Salt Lake City, is the largest open-pit copper mine in the world, and looks like Paul Bunyan's fingerprint. It is two miles across, a half mile deep, and only one of the vast operations of the Kennecott Copper Corporation's Utah Copper Division. The ore is blasted from the sides of the mine (called benches), scooped up in 30-ton bites by huge electric shovels, and dumped into one of the many ore trains that circle the benches on moveable tracks or into huge haulage trucks at the upper levels. From there it is taken by 100-car ore trains over a private electric railroad to the processing plants at Magna, sixteen miles away. Visitors are invited to watch the huge earth-shaking blasts from an observation platform nearby.

THE COLORADO RIVER carves a gorge through the sandstone buttes near Dead Horse Point at Moab, in eastern Utah. In these canyons banking the Colorado and Green rivers lies some of the most spectacular scenery in the West including the Arches National Monument. Much of this land was inaccessible, except by horse or Jeep, until the great uranium hunt just after World War II, when many trails and dirt tracks were broadened and made passable for cars. Some enterprising prospectors even carved small airstrips on the treeless plateaus, but even today venturesome tourists are still advised to bring water and basic supplies before entering the canyonlands. Moab, the principal town, has fet the growing pains caused by prospectors, uranium finds and other mineral discoveries.

JACKSON LAKE AND THE GRAND TETON MOUNTAINS form a breathtaking vista in northwestern Wyoming. The Tetons spread across a 40-mile strip of Rocky Mountains, have more than 22 peaks cresting 10,000 feet, and the tallest in the range is Grand Teton, soaring 13,766 feet high. The Snake River, starting above Jackson Lake, continues south through a flat fertile valley that is a large elk feeding area, and then abruptly swings to the northwest, eventually to join the Columbia River. Jackson Hole is the name given to the entire basin, and it has become a popular vacation area in summer and ski center in winter. Situated just south of Yellowstone Park, Jackson Hole was once established as a National Monument, but in 1950 it became part of the Grand Teton National Park.

AN ALFALFA FARM in the Snake River Valley below Jackson Hole spreads like a thick green carpet over this fertile basin. The farms are smaller than those farther east, but are highly productive owing to plentiful water from the Tetons' year-round snows.

THE SNAKE RIVER winds through the bottomland below Jackson Hole before turning westward through Idaho. The Snake is a major tributary of the Columbia, and its course was followed by the early settlers moving westward to the California gold fields.

DOWNTOWN LAS VEGAS AT NIGHT is illuminated by thousands of bright lights that adorn the gambling casinos of this resort city in the southern end of the state. While it may be hard to believe, Las Vegas was first settled by the Mormons in 1855; they gave up two years later, leaving us to wonder if they knew something we didn't. In 1911, the city was chartered; in addition to the obvious attractions of the casinos and gambling halls, there is a solid core of ranching and mining activity surrounding it. In fact, the population has more than doubled since World War II; and while much of this growth is tied to the entertainment industry, a sizable stable working force has also developed that has caught the eyes of industrialists, particularly in the aerospace field. Recent property acquisitions suggest a definite future for Las Vegas in the coming supersonic world.

THE LAS VEGAS STRIP, outside the city's limits, has become a major center of opulent hotels and entertainment places, and attracts thousands of people who come as much for the sun, sand, and hot, dry climate as they do for the slot machines and dice tables. A huge new convention hall and exhibit area have done much to turn this into a major convention site drawing mainly from the business world of the West. While the City of Las Vegas is built along vertical lines in a manner befitting a downtown area, the new hotels along the strip are sprawled over huge acreages including high-rise units, bubbling fountains, numerous swimming pools, lavish restaurants that somehow seem to negate themselves by catering to a diet-conscious clientele, and, of course, the round-the-clock casinos that seem to be as busy at nine in the morning as they are at night.

154

THE HOTEL TROPICANA, typical of the Las Vegas hostelries on the Strip, offers a broad variety of entertainment, sports, elegant shops, and the ever-present gambling rooms.

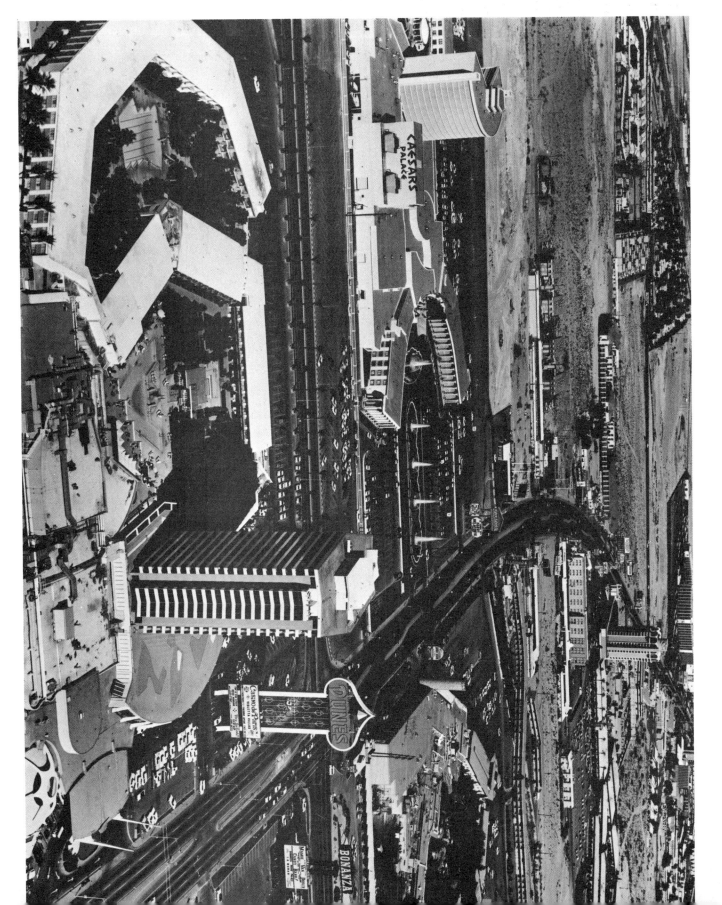

HOOVER DAM on the lower Colorado River is one of the great engineering works of man. Located in Black Canyon, twenty-five miles from Las Vegas, it supplies power, water, and recreational facilities to much of the Southwest. First called Boulder Dam when finished in 1936, even by today's standards its dimensions are impressive: 660 feet thick at the base, 726 feet high, and with a crest almost quarter of a mile long. Nearby is Boulder City, first laid out to house the construction workers and now used by the U.S. Bureau of Reclamation.

LAKE MEAD is formed by the backup of the Colorado River at Hoover Dam, and has become one of the best national watersites in the country. Covering an area of more than 3,000 square miles, it provides a huge recreation area for boating, fishing, and swimming, and follows the Colorado River for 115 miles almost to the Grand Canyon.

THE BIGGEST LITTLE CITY IN THE WORLD is what Reno, Nevada, calls itself, and proudly proclaims this from overhead signs on South Virginia Street, the gateway to the main strip of casinos and entertainment spots. But Reno has grown to be a lot more than a neon-lit gambling center, and is now developing as an import warehousing and distributing complex for the Mountain West. The University of Nevada is located here, and is noted for its highly respected Mackay School of Mines and the Atmospherium, which are doing important basic research in environmental factors affecting the atmosphere and related problems of outer space.

THE TRUCKEE RIVER VALLEY, just east of the Donner Pass between California and Nevada, is fertile bottomland fed by the Truckee, which comes out of the mountains around Lake Tahoe. A broad interstate highway now threads its way through the pass, paralleled by the tracks of the Southern Pacific Railroad. But it wasn't always easy to get through, as the Donner party found out in the winter of 1846 when they became stranded by heavy snow, and near starvation reduced some to cannibalism. Only 47 of the original 89 in the party survived, and these had to be brought out by rescue teams from Fort Sutter, now Sacramento.

VIRGINIA CITY ONCE BOASTED of the only elevator between Chicago and San Francisco, and in its heyday as a mining center its ratio of six churches to 110 saloons serving a population of 30,000 speaks for itself. Once a roaring, lusty silver town, whose fame was established by the discovery of the bonanza called the Comstock Lode in 1859, Virginia City (below) became the symbol of the booming West, complete with its own opera house. A castle built in 1868 by Robert Graves was furnished with priceless antiques from all over the world, and is now a museum open to the public. Today, tourists are the town's main industry.

LAKE TAHOE STRADDLING the Nevada-California line is a lovely mountain lake 22 miles long, 15 miles wide, and 1,600 feet deep, most of which is in California, though because of the gambling laws the more popular hotels and casinos are just over the Nevada line. The lake, which is at an altitude of 6,225 feet in the heart of the Sierra Nevada, is ringed by snow-capped peaks rising an additional 4,000 feet. Three national forests, Tahoe, Eldorado, and Toiyabe, almost surround the lake, making it ideal for both summer and winter sports, as well as for the indoor sports offered by casinos and lodges on the eastern end.

160

The Northwest

EIGHTEEN MONTHS AFTER THEY LEFT St. Louis, United States Army Captains Meriwether Lewis and William Clark arrived at the mouth of the Columbia River and saw the Pacific Ocean, and American history will not forget that November day in 1805, when the way to the Northwest became a reality. Before many years passed, the settlers would be streaming westward along the Oregon Trail, some heading northwest along the Snake River, others turning south at a fork in Idaho to get to the gold country of northern California.

Those who pushed on along the Snake came into the Big Bend of the Columbia and saw the lush bottomland, tall timber, and the great Cascade Range with its towering snow-covered peaks. Other settlers moved along the seaboard from California, and established forts at the many bays and inlets that dotted the coastline. Juan de Fuca Strait provided a deepwater passage for ocean shipping into protected Puget Sound. And Seattle, Tacoma, and Olympia, though miles from the ocean, still became thriving seaports. Across the river from Fort Vancouver, Portland was established, and all these busy harbors soon became shipping centers for lumber, fish, fruit, vegetables and, later, pulp, paper, and aluminum.

While some of the needs of the Northwest were dissimilar to those of Tennessee Valley, the necessity for power and flood control was apparent, and just as the TVA brought industry into the Appalachians, so did the establishment of the large hydro-electric plants stimulate the growth of industry in Washington and Oregon.

When airplanes were in their fledgling stages, their wooden frames were built from the strong and supple spruce of Northwest forests, and the Boeing Airplane Company was founded here. And though aluminum alloys have replaced the wood in modern jet liners, Boeing continues its production in the Seattle area, and the aircraft industry is as much a part of the Northwest as are the sawmills and pulp mills.

The ever-present water helped establish the early economy of the Northwest, and its influence is enormous. Everything seems related to or dependent upon the water. The two major bridges crossing Lake Washington are floating bridges; the vast docks can accommodate over a hundred oceangoing vessels at one time; and the nearby rivers and fishing ports supply millions of pounds of salmon and other seafood every year. Logs are floated down the rivers in huge rafts and tied up in the lumber mill basins of Tacoma, Olympia, Portland, and Coos Bay.

Most of this activity takes place along a narrow swath west of the Cascades, the huge mountains cleaving the Northwest into two distinct areas. Though the mountains are breached by passes that carry rivers, railroads, and highways, the two regions greatly differ not only in economy but in appearance as well. On the west slope are the verdant greens of the forests watered by the heavy rains that sweep in from the ocean and form the snows that keep the higher peaks perpetually whitened. The range is spectacular, with six mountains topping the 10,000-foot mark, providing the setting for the huge National Forests. As in the Northeast, skiing has become a way of life, with trails, slopes, chair lifts, and lodges dotting the entire range. By far the most popular resort is the year-round Snoqualmie Ski Area nestling in the middle of the 1,200,000-acre Snoqualmie National Forest, forty-six miles from Seattle.

On the east slope of the range the terrain changes abruptly. The rivers form the backbones for the large fruit and wheat farms in the valleys, but away from the river the land is dry, and earth-colored in contrast to the west slope.

The chief artery, of course, is the mighty Columbia River, bridged by the many hydroelectric dams that create the deep pools to make the river navigable for barge shipping. Each of the dams has a fish ladder, an ingenious series of steps that become miniature waterfalls so that the salmon can get upstream to their spawning grounds in the headwaters of the river.

But in the Northwest, as in so many other sections of the country, man has rushed to strip the land of its wealth, with little reflection on what might happen to that land for future generations. Forests have been cut over, burned, and brutally slashed, ruining some growths forever and destroying stands of timber that will not be replaced in many lifetimes. Like the cypress of the Gulf South, the redwoods and other great firs have become the rallying point for conservationists who plead for a halt in the cutting before this species is gone forever. Only in recent years has the practice of selective logging taken place, and reseeding of the faster-growing varieties has been hurried along by the use of helicopters.

Second in devastation to the lands has been the devastation to the air, particularly in the Tacoma area, where the pulp mills and wood-refuse burners belch the nauseating smoke that blights the countryside for miles around. Some residents feel that before long this pollution may be an academic question, because if a halt is not called to the rapacious logging that reseeding has not equaled, then, in time, there may not be any more timber to convert to pulp, plywood, and paper, and a wooden floor or wood-paneled room may become an artifact of this century to be classed with Model "T" Ford flivvers or high button shoes.

THE DOCKS AT SEATTLE are the gathering places for ships from all the world that take out the lumber, food, and manufactures of the Northwest and bring in products and raw materials from Europe, Africa, and the Orient.

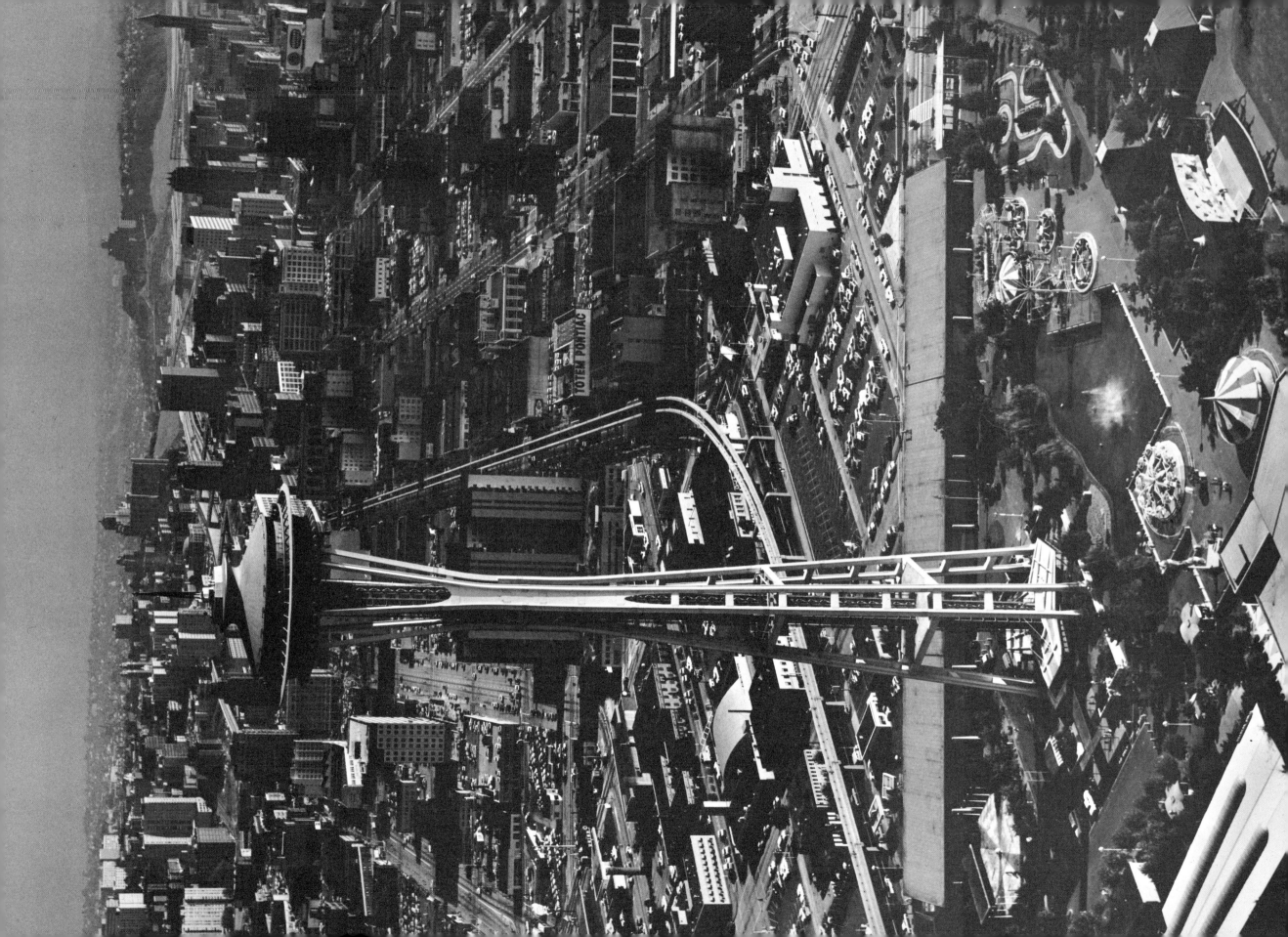

SEATTLE'S SPACE NEEDLE, constructed for the World's Fair of 1962 and now a permanent part of the city's skyline, is an eye-catching structure 607 feet high and topped with a revolving-dome restaurant and observation deck. From its viewing points, the visitor gets a complete panoramic view of the most important city in the Pacific Northwest. Seattle is a water city, with Puget Sound on one side and Lake Washington on the other. Freighters, ferryboats, sailboats, and powerboats keep the big harbor busy with world trade, commuters, and pleasure seekers. Seattle Center at the base of the Space Needle is an attractive area of shops, restaurants, exhibits, and a theatre and opera house, all originally constructed for the fair but now part of the permanent scene. A monorail carries passengers from downtown.

MODERN BUILDINGS IN DOWNTOWN Seattle range from the new IBM Building to the adjacent Plymouth Congressional Church, both of which are extremely distinctive and in keeping with the get-up-and-go attitude of the Northwesterners. Sometimes the spirit of progress runs away with itself, as it did in the case of the big freeway that split the city in half and raised a furor of controversy that only now is dying down (see next page). As in the case of the San Francisco Embarcadero Freeway after it was built, the people of Seattle suddenly realized what had happened to their beautiful city, and immediately a howl of protest arose to deck it over, bury it, or tear it up altogether. None of this happened, and the cars continue to whiz by in ever-increasing numbers, carrying heavy streams of traffic north and south.

163

THE SEATTLE FREEWAY, a ten-lane race-track through the heart of the city, effectively splits the metropolis in half and turns into an instant parking lot when some unwary motorist becomes confused by the lane di-viders and promptly ends up perched on one until the rescue crews arrive to pry him off.

THE EVERGREEN POINT Floating Bridge across Lake Washington is somewhat less hazardous than the freeway, presuming the motorist knows how to swim. This is the world's longest floating bridge, a mile and a half in length, supported by floating pontoons and joining downtown Seattle to its suburbs.

MOUNT RAINIER, southeast of Tacoma, is the tallest peak in the Cascades, rising to 14,410 feet above sea level. Permanently snow-capped and spawning six glaciers in its summit alone, it stands in the heart of Mount Rainier National Park, a heavily forested preserve whose tree line is 6,400 feet up. Above the tree line are the cirques, the area between 10,000 and 12,000 feet where the snow is heaviest and glaciers are born.

THE GRAND CANYON AND TAOS PUEBLO are nature's and man's separate monuments to time in the Southwest, their earth colors reflecting the traditional hues of the region. At the left, the Colorado River winds through the bottom of the canyon that wind and water took thousands of years to carve. The Pueblo (above), estimated to be at least 800 years old, is much the same as it was 400 years ago when the Spaniards saw it as they first explored North America.

FISHERMAN'S WHARF IN SAN FRANCISCO is an intricate center of docks, fishing boats, shops, and restaurants patronized by tourists and local residents. In the background is the Embarcadero, San Francisco's famous deepwater piers that serve oceangoing traffic from all over the world. The Bay Bridge is at the top.

THE SUGARCANE FIELDS of Hawaii on the Island of Kauai blanket the land with green, extending to the mountains. The trade winds, carrying moisture from the sea, condense on the cooler land masses into the plentiful rainfall that makes this rich red earth so productive. Pineapple growing is also extensive on the island.

THE LIGHTS OF RENO blaze from sundown to sunup, and even at high noon, as the busy casinos draw the gamblers and kibitzers to the slot machines and the blackjack tables.

California

CALIFORNIA, SOME HUMORISTS have said, is not a state but a condition, and even native Californians often agree—to some extent, that is. The third largest state in the Union (after Alaska and Texas) and the largest in population, California is big enough and varied enough and populated enough to be a region by itself. Extending some 800 miles up from Mexico to Oregon, and averaging some 235 miles in width, it is spectacularly varied in terrain and climate. It can claim the highest and lowest points within the original 48 states. Its enormous recreational areas (25 million acres of public lands), magnificent climate, and tremendous natural resources certainly are reason enough for its nickname of the Golden State.

Like the rest of the Pacific Coast states, California is divided longitudinally by mountains. The Cascade Range spreads south below the Oregon border to join the Sierra Nevada near Mount Lassen, the last active volcano in the contiguous United States, which erupted as late as 1921. From there the Sierra Nevada ranges southward through Yosemite and Sequoia National parks, and from there Mount Whitney stands supreme down into the Mojave Desert.

The coastal regions are equally spectacular. The beautiful beaches of southern California, flanked by the Coastal Range, spread all the way through the Big Sur to Monterey and San Francisco. North of the Golden Gate are the Redwoods and the timber-producing areas around Eureka, which is the biggest port between San Francisco and the mouth of the Columbia River.

California's population grew from many sources, starting with the first Spanish exploration about 1540, followed by an English expedition led by Sir Francis Drake in 1579, and succeeded by other Spanish and English explorers. But real colonization began when the twenty-one Spanish missions were established along El Camino Real, a six-hundred-mile road running from San Diego to Sonoma. After years of Spanish and Mexican rule, and including a brief period as an independent republic, the area became a United States possession in the late 1840's, and a state in 1850.

Before statehood, however, rumors about the riches of the new California country had already seeped eastward, and pioneers started streaming west over the Oregon Trail by every available means—horse-drawn wagons, mules, on foot, and by ship around Cape Horn. One party of eighty-nine people tried crossing the Sierra Nevada in the winter of 1846, to become stranded and trapped in the icy mountains. Of the group, forty-seven survived, and, according to some historians, only after resorting to cannibalism. This was the famous Donner Party that tried to get through the pass of the Truckee River but was stopped by the sheer mountain walls that necessitated lowering their wagons and supplies, piece by piece, by rope down the cliffs. Just two years after that, in 1848, gold was discovered on

the lands of Captain John Sutter, and the following year brought the stampede of the forty-niners. But many prospectors never found the gold, and turned to farming, lumbering, and fishing. Others stayed in the ports to create the cities and build the railroads that soon were threading both East and West.

After the turn of the century two new ingredients were injected—movies and the automobile—but many more years were to pass before either of them became the hallmarks of the state that they are today. The necessity for shooting outdoors with primitive equipment required a fine climate that could be depended upon throughout the year. Later, however, as new filming techniques developed, the great studios moved indoors, particularly after the addition of sound, which required more controlled conditions than could be provided on the back lot of a movie studio.

Similarly the automobile came into its own in a big way, particularly in southern California, where the distances were vast and Los Angeles grew too rapidly ever to establish a comprehensive rapid transit system. The threat of earthquakes in northern California similarly prevented the building of subways, already overcrowded in New York.

After World War II, freeways began growing and clawing their way through miles of residential areas, symbolic of the routes to be taken by the future legless American who never walks anywhere he cannot drive.

Today San Francisco has become the focal point of the Californians who felt that the freeways have gone too far and too fast. Barely had the new elevated freeway around the Embarcadero been finished when horrified San Franciscans realized they could hardly see their beloved Ferry Building at the foot of Market Street. A clamor resulted, which has not been resolved, to tear down the unsightly freeway and perhaps bar automobiles entirely from some of the more crowded areas of this beautiful city. And a Bay Area Rapid Transit System has been started, which, though beset by the difficulties of distance, financing, and design, surely must be the only solution to prevent the city from choking itself to death with automobiles. And the cable cars clank on, those anachronistic throwbacks to the turn of the century, which the tourists love and which the permanent residents profess to hate—until a suggestion is made that they be eliminated.

So far, the magnificent coastline from Monterey down to Point Sur is more or less unspoiled, though oil rigs are now creeping out into the water farther south, with an attempt in some cases, as in the Long Beach area, to disguise them as high-rise buildings. But the cities retain their individual flavor: Los Angeles continues to sprawl with increasing growing pains, and San Francisco tries desperately to preserve its Victorian charm; Berkeley has its students, and the visitors have their Disneyland.

181

SHASTA DAM on the Sacramento River in northern California. Like Hoover and Grand Coulee dams, it ranks among the greatest works of America's builders. Water stored here is distributed well into the southern part of the Central Valley for irrigation purposes.

SAN FRANCISCO

THE FERRY BUILDING at the foot of Market Street is a beloved landmark of San Francisco. Often called the Paris of the West, a plan was actually devised to reconstruct the city along Parisian lines, but the earthquake of 1906 and the subsequent rush to rebuild forced the planners to shelve such grandiose ideas and reconstruct the city in a more conventional manner. Often fog-shrouded, a bank of fog can be seen in the background rolling in from the nearby Pacific Ocean.

THE SAN FRANCISCO–OAKLAND Bridge leaps across San Francisco Bay in a giant double step, pausing on Yerbe Buena Island before continuing across to the East Bay cities of Oakland, Berkeley, and Richmond. Ten lanes of heavy auto, bus, and truck traffic are carried on its two broad decks.

TELEGRAPH HILL AND COIT TOWER, dual landmarks in San Francisco and a monument to the firemen of the great conflagration of 1906 that followed the earthquake, afford the visitor a splendid view of the city. In the background is the Embarcadero and the Bay Bridge on the city's waterfront. At the right is the Golden Gateway, a redevelopment of the old waterfront district near North Beach.

THE TENDERLOIN DISTRICT (right) is another of San Francisco's once colorful downtown areas having its heyday in the gold rush of the 1850's. Edging the downtown shopping area and the financial district, it has a number of small fine hotels such as the Olympic in the foreground, and big chain-operated hotels like the opulent Hilton behind it. Some first-rate restaurants are in this area.

NOB HILL (lower right), one of the finer hotel and residential districts of San Francisco, boasts many of the better-known hosteleries such as the Mark Hopkins and Fairmount hotels (lower left). California Street, between the two hotels, is still serviced by a cable car that skirts the edge of Chinatown (extreme left). In the background are the Ferry Building, financial district, and the Bay Bridge.

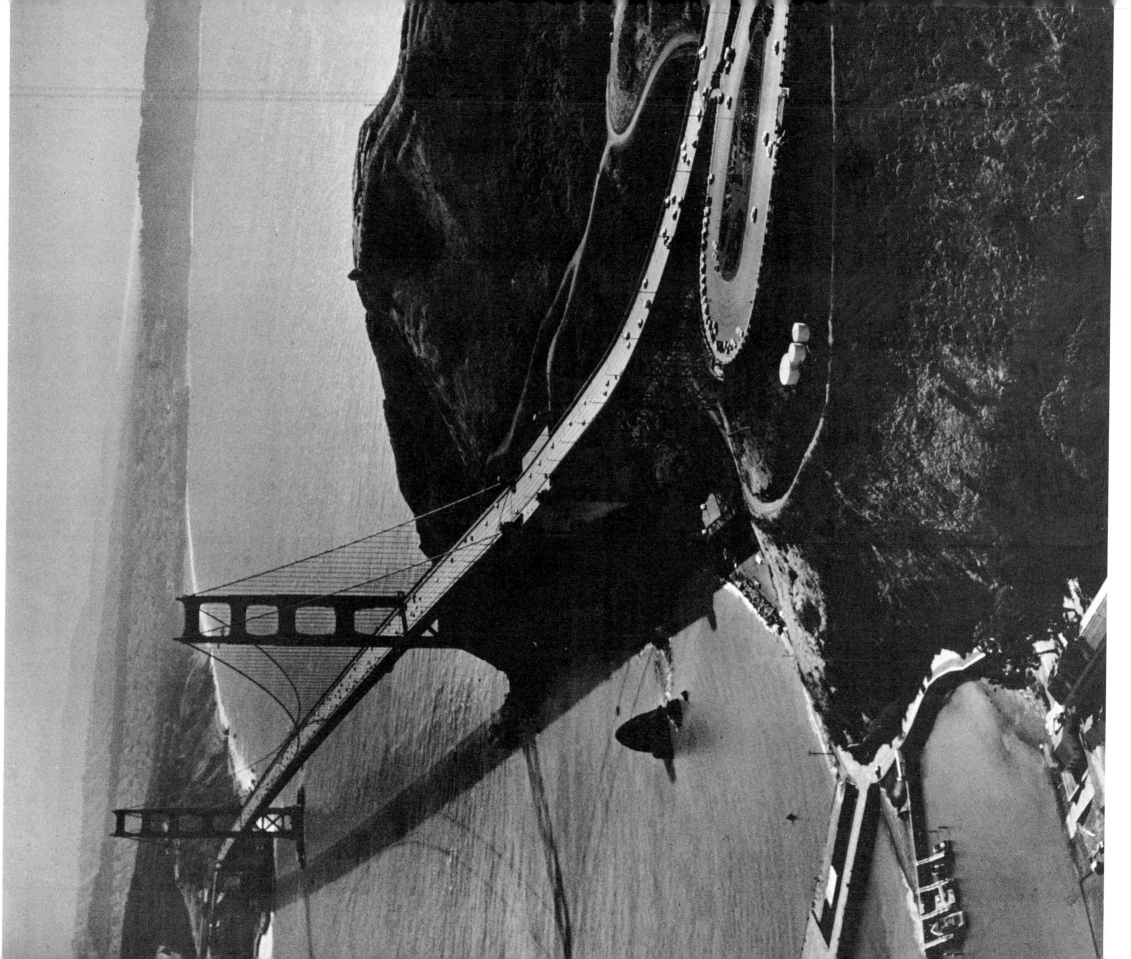

GHIRARDELLI SQUARE, once a chocolate factory in the Fisherman's Wharf area, and now a charming shopping center of small arts and crafts shops, boutiques and restaurants, is one of a series of developments that utilize older structures for newer ideas. Another popular place is The Cannery, similarly converted into a complex of shops and restaurants, including an Elizabethan pub with antique paneling.

THE GOLDEN GATE BRIDGE between San Francisco and Marin County across the Golden Gate sweeps over the entrance to San Francisco Bay. One of the largest single-span suspension bridges ever built, its main span is 4,200 feet long and carries traffic 220 feet above the water. In the foreground is a lookout point on the Marin County side with an excellent view of the Bay, Angel and Alcatraz Islands, and the city itself. On the other side is Sea Cliff Beach, a popular picnic, swimming, and sunbathing area of six acres facing the Pacific Ocean.

THE PALACE OF FINE ARTS, originally built for the Panama-Pacific Exposition of 1915, and left to decay, has been restored to its original glory down to the ducks and swans swimming in its lagoons. It is located near the Presidio, the historic U.S. Army reservation.

MARINA GREEN, a pleasant greensward at the foot of Baker Street and near the Presidio, is the gathering place for all San Franciscans who want to walk a dog, fly a kite, sunbathe, play volleyball, girl-watch, or escape from North Beach, Haight-Ashbury, or even the rarefied atmosphere of Russian Hill or Nob Hill. The main requirements are a blanket to stretch out on, some sun, and plenty of time to do nothing at all.

SAUSALITO IN MARIN COUNTY across the Golden Gate Bridge is a mixture of Greenwich Village and Darien or Westport, with psychedelic bookstores, arts and crafts shops, mingled with quaint restaurants and fleets of small boats moored among the hulks of the retired ferries that used to ply across San Francisco Bay. The houses perched on the steep hillsides have their backs to the dense fogs that often roll in.

190

OAKLAND

OAKLAND, CALIFORNIA, has become a West Coast Megalopolis separated from the rest of the cities in Alameda County by only a thin line of demarcation, yet it is quite an attractive city. In its center is Lake Merritt, a large saltwater tidal lake that is fed by a connection to San Francisco Bay. The large building in the foreground is the Kaiser Center, corporate headquarters of the vast Kaiser Corporation, a leading West Coast company that has pioneered in social programs for its employees and families. Oakland also has a pleasant waterfront area called Jack London Square, named in honor of the California-born writer whose books reflected much of the temper of the gold-rush era.

BERKELEY

THE UNIVERSITY OF CALIFORNIA at Berkeley is one of the largest in the world, with a total enrollment of about 55,000 students, approximately 22,000 of whom attend this campus on the east side of San Francisco Bay. While Berkeley offers an enormous variety of courses, much of its most important work has been in scientific research, especially in the field of nuclear physics, which it has probed extensively since 1930. Only part of the vast campus is visible here: the 307-foot-high Campanile, the 80,000-seat California Memorial Stadium (upper right), Edwards Field athletic center (right).

194

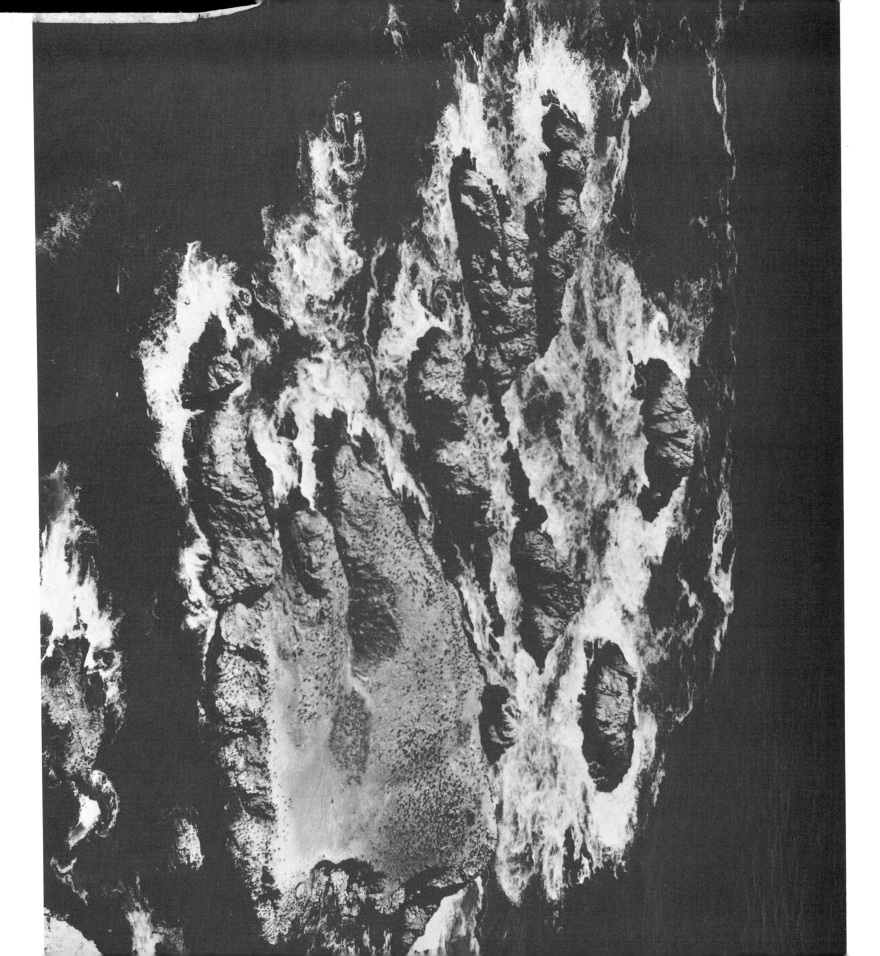

BIG SUR

THE BIG SUR COUNTRY is an incredibly beautiful strip of Pacific Ocean coastline from Monterey south, dotted with great rocks jutting out of the crashing seas or with sheer cliffs dropping down to the water's edge. Close by are the Santa Lucia Mountains, part of the Coastal Range, all of which blend spectacularly to form a backdrop of roaring surf, craggy rocks, and subtly colored seaweed. The rocks are alive with water birds who nest there and fish the water, and often the California sea lions clamber up to sun themselves or raid a sea gull nest.

POINT LOBOS on the California Coast near Monterey has been immortalized by famed photographer Edward Weston, who spent the better part of a lifetime photographing this area. Seen here from the ocean side, the point juts out into the sea, and the Santa Lucia Mountains rise majestically behind it.

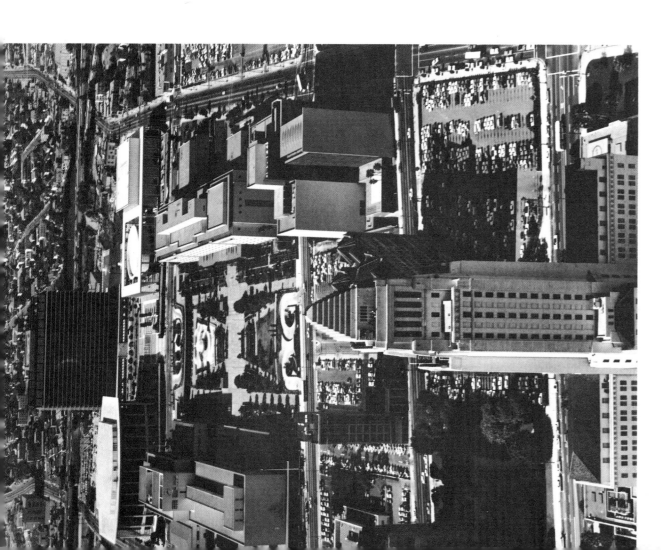

THE CIVIC CENTER AND MUSIC CENTER (above) are the showcases of Los Angeles, largest city in California and third largest in the country. The building in the foreground is the City Hall, once the tallest in town since an old ordinance restricted buildings to a height of thirteen stories. When this restriction was lifted in 1957, skyscrapers started sprouting all over the city, mainly toward the Wilshire District. In the background is the Music Center for the Performing Arts, a handsome three-building complex consisting of the Mark Taper Forum, the Ahmanson Theatre, the Chandler Pavilion, and other public buildings.

WILSHIRE AND SANTA MONICA BOULEVARDS intersect in Beverly Hills, and the sprawling mass that is Los Angeles covers hundreds of square miles in all directions. On these two heavily trafficked thoroughfares, new buildings rise almost daily, and the automobile is the great common denominator, with parking lots scattered on every available rooftop, backyard, and other unbuilt-upon space. Yet the geographic and administrative center of the city is a good ten miles to the east, and will, in effect, move farther eastward as the westward drive continues with even more high-rise apartments, office buildings, and hotels.

A SMOG-FILLED CANYON in Hollywood Hills, typical habitat of the cliff-climbing species who live on Outpost Drive in this western part of Los Angeles. Their building cycle is as predictable as that of the beaver or bird, quite different from the cliff dwellers in the East who live in a different type of nest called an apartment house. First a bulldozer gouges out a deep slash in the canyon wall, and then, because of the nest in front, a new structure is erected on a higher set of stilts, or hung a little more precariously on the cliff wall. Then a swimming pool is dug out of the soft ground, some vines or shrubs are planted, and the new abode is occupied. Somewhat later, a brush fire roars up the canyon or a mud slide slithers down, the structures are wiped out, and the building cycle starts over again

Hawaii

2,400 MILES WEST OF SAN FRANCISCO, and spread out over 1,600 miles of Pacific Ocean, are the Hawaiian Islands, a chain of eight main islands and some smaller islets, reefs, and atolls that make up our lush and beautiful fiftieth state.

Historians say the islands were probably first inhabited by Polynesians about the tenth century C.E., but as far as the Western world is concerned, 1778 was the year of its discovery by Captain Cook. After that, Hawaii existed as an independent kingdom ruled by King Kamehameha, later became a republic, then a possession of the United States in 1898, receiving territorial status two years afterward. It achieved statehood in 1959.

The islands are varied, with active volcanoes and mountains reaching as high as 13,825 feet above sea level. There are black lava beds, sandy beaches, and luxuriant rain forests; the earth is rich, and sugarcane and pineapple are the dominant crops, though cattle raising is extensive.

Most activity centers on Oahu, which holds the City of Honolulu and the huge military installations of Pearl Harbor and Hickam Field, in addition to the landmarks of Diamond Head, the Punchbowl (now a national cemetery), and Koko Head. The big hotels cluster around Waikiki Beach, a surprisingly small piece of real estate when one considers its fame.

The Port of Honolulu is the gateway to the islands, and while airplanes probably handle more passengers, those who arrive by ship are greeted by traditional ukulele bands and lei-clad hula dancers throwing hibiscus. These visitors usually get their first glimpse of Hawaii as the ships pass Diamond Head en route to the harbor entrance. Aside from the general island mass rising from the sea, the second landmark seen by a new arrival is the Aloha Tower on the waterfront of the City of Honolulu. Beyond this tower the mountains of the Koolau Range sweep up 3,150 feet from the coastal plain. Bulldozers having cleared what was once dense undergrowth, houses have rooted along the sides of the mountain range instead. The Nuuanu Pali Pass pierces the range and is now threaded by a broad highway carrying the bulk of the commuter traffic over the mountain to Kaneohe and Kailua, the principal residential areas of Oahu. And a new Interstate Highway threads its way behind Honolulu, carrying traffic from the Pearl Harbor areas toward Koko Head.

Of the other islands, each has its own spectacular characteristics. Hawaii, or the "Big Island," is the largest of the entire group, and contains the still live Kilauea and Mauna Loa volcanoes. Kilauea, more active of the two, rises only a little above 4,000 feet, but its rim is accessible by car, and when it erupts, as it does periodically, the proximity to a highway probably makes it the most observed and photographed active volcano in the world.

The Big Island is covered with lava beds that have flowed for years from active craters and that, through time, have turned many colors. In some places, such as the Kona Coast, the lava beds reach into the sea to form a spectacular contrast with the iridescent ocean. The northeast side of Hawaii, like the rest of the islands, gets the trade winds carrying moisture from the sea, with the result that the sugarcane grows like a thick carpet.

Because of its location on a beautiful bay, the small city of Hilo has seen an upsurge of tourism, and has responded by building a number of fine hotels and a jetport. The other large islands are Kauai, with its rain forest, Waimea Canyon, and multihued Napali Cliffs. Maui has the spectacular crater of Haleakala situated in a National Park. The other islands of Molokai, Lanai, and Kahoolawe all lie between Oahu and Hawaii.

Notwithstanding the spectacular geography, rich pineapple and sugar plantations, and shining beaches, the most beautiful asset of Hawaii is generally considered to be the people. All races live here and all cultures, and nowhere in the United States do they live together more harmoniously, though there are still a few who try desperately by social and economic pressures to enforce separation.

Even today, while many of the old social and racial prejudices still exist, for most Hawaiians this provincialism ended when Pearl Harbor was attacked on December 7, 1941. Tragic as it was, this was a unifying force, for the heroic battle acquittal of the Japanese-Americans served notice to the world that love of country far transcended blood origins.

Hawaii's heritage stems from Polynesians, Chinese, Japanese, and U.S. mainlanders, plus travelers who remained after seeing the beauty of the islands. Their cultures give the islands their vibrancy and stimulus, setting them apart from all other tropic and semitropic islands of the world, whether east or west.

201

THE NA PALI CLIFFS in the wilderness area of northwestern Kauai drop precipitously to tiny little beaches that can be reached only by helicopter or a skillful boatman. The tops of these cliffs are almost always covered by low clouds that condense on the land mass and provide the moisture for the lush vegitation growing in the spectacular Waimea Canyon on the southwestern side.

THE LUXURY LINER "ORIANA," pride of the P & O Lines, lies in port alongside the Aloha Tower, famous landmark of Honolulu on the island of Oahu. The modern business district of the city rises behind the piers, and in the background is the extinct volcano called the Punchbowl, now used as the site of the National Memorial Cemetery of the Pacific. Honolulu is the largest city of the Hawaiian Islands and is the growing center for both commerce and tourism for all Hawaii.

THE MOUNTAINS OF KAUAI rise from the sea on the northwestern shore. Kauai is considered to be the oldest of the Hawaiian chain, and Mount Waialeale in its center is supposed to be the wettest spot in the world, receiving some 460 inches or more of rain annually on its windward side. On all sides of the island are lovely beaches, and on the rich red earth of the fertile plains are the highly productive fields of pineapple and sugarcane, the island's main economic mainstay.

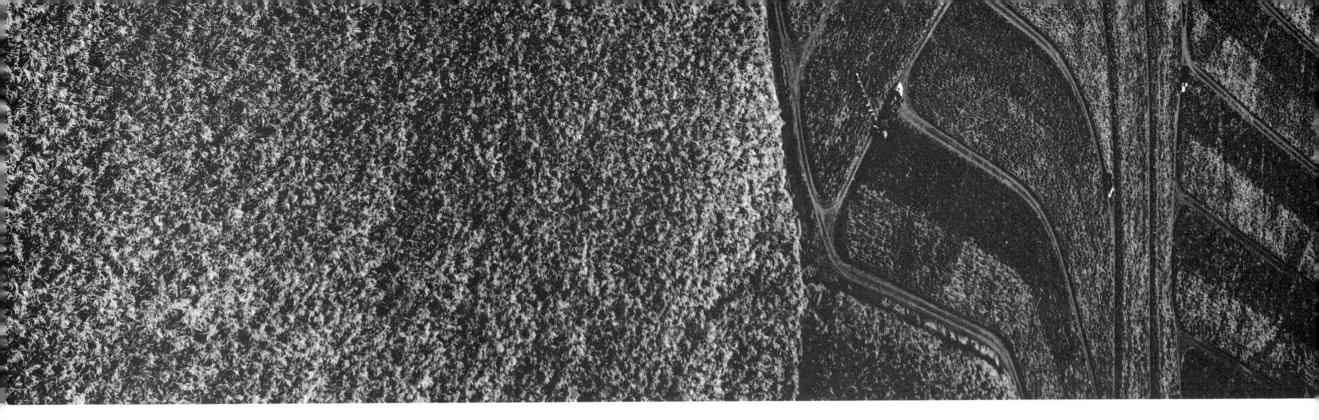

THE PINEAPPLE AND SUGARCANE FIELDS of Kauai form interlocking patterns on the low plains along the coast as the fields are laid out to permit the use of mechanical seeders and harvesters. The field in the upper part of the picture is being worked with machinery, while the field in the upper left and the sugar field below it have yet to be harvested.

THE ISLAND OF HAWAII, or the "Big Island," lies some 300 miles to the southeast of Kauai at the other end of the string, and it too has the lush sugarcane that grows on the windward side of the islands. This sugar plantation on the north shore of Hawaii comes down to the cliff's very edge, and the cane blankets the land with a thick green mantle. Hawaii's largest city, Hilo, is only a few miles east, and a growing tourist center.

208

THE CRATER MOUTH AT KILAUE on Hawaii, less than an hour's drive from Hilo, is another gathering place for the tourist, since an excellent access road brings one right to the very rim of this still-active volcano. Kilaue is at the base of Mauna Loa, the great volcano that rises to 13,680 feet; Mauna Kea, its nearby sister peak, rises even higher, to 13,825 feet, making it the loftiest in all the Hawaiian Islands. On the opposite side of the island is the spectacular Kona Coast with its small city of Kailua and the famous black lava flows to the sea.

TOURISM AND WAIKIKI BEACH ARE SYNONYMOUS in Hawaii; and, though ringed by excellent hotels, the beaches themselves are very much in the public domain. Moreover, property owners bordering the beach sites must maintain a clearly marked access way for the public at large. Thus these sands become the friendliest in the world, with an easy intermingling that makes for instant camaraderie.

209

A SURFER RIDES A BIG ONE into the beach at Waikiki in this thrilling sport that challenges everyone who has tried it. In the background, three other surfers jockey their boards into position to catch the next rollers.

Index

211